A Literary Tour Guide to the United States: NORTHEAST

Americans Discover America Series

A Literary Tour Guide to the United States: NORTHEAST

BY EMILIE C. HARTING

WILLIAM MORROW AND COMPANY, INC.
NEW YORK   1978

Library of Congress Cataloging in Publication Data

Harting, Emilie C
   A literary tour guide to the United States.

   1. Literary landmarks—Northeastern States.
2. Authors, American—Homes and haunts.   3. North-
eastern States—Description and travel—Guide-books.
I. Title.
PS144.N65H3   917.4′04′4   77–18439
ISBN 0-688-03281-8
ISBN 0-688-08281-5 travelflex

Printed in the United States of America.

First Edition

1   2   3   4   5   6   7   8   9   10

To fellow literary pilgrims—
Rob,
Morgan,
and Thea.

PREFACE

This book is a guide for those interested in reading about or visiting places associated with authors, most major, a few minor. It is not, however, intended as an atlas or gazetteer of locales appearing in literary works. The general criterion for inclusion in this book is that a place be visible and open to the public at least part of the year.

Please keep in mind that while every attempt has been made to include the most accurate and up-to-date data on open buildings, visiting hours are always subject to change.

CONTENTS

CONNECTICUT

Cos Cob

Bush-Holley House (39 Strickland Rd., off US 1. Open 10-noon and 2-5, Tues.-Sat.; 2-4 Sun. Adm. charged). This was the Holley Inn in the late 1800s. Run by Emma Constant Holley and her husband, the famous sculptor Elmer Livingston MacRae, it was a Cos Cob art colony where genteel writers, painters, editors, and publishers came to relax in the peaceful country atmosphere and enjoy the hospitality of the Holley family. Now the headquarters of the Greenwich Historical Society, the gracious old house is filled with fine Colonial antiques and artwork donated by the Bush and Holley families and others in the area.

In his *Autobiography,* Lincoln Steffens, a frequent guest, called the house a "beautiful old accident—so old that it had its slave quarters up under the roof; and it looked out from under the elms as high as oaks upon the inner harbor and an abandoned boat-building house with sail lofts. There was a long veranda where the breezes blew down from the river, up from the Sound, and cooled the debaters and settled the dinner debates . . ." Besides Steffens, Willa ·Cather, and Anya Seton, who also wrote about the house, there were a number of artists who came here and painted it. When the Society bought the building in 1957, they used those writers' and artists' impressions as records to guide them in the restoration.

Novelist Anya Seton developed her interest in writing here when she visited as a child. She often came to play with the Holley children and was intrigued by the conversations that their father had with the guests. The children played in the dark cellar with its secret passageways and creaky trap doors. Those experiences became part of her novels.

At that time there was no thoroughfare at the bottom of the hill and trees were all that separated the house from Long Island Sound. It was always breezy and the smell of the undeveloped marshes in Cos Cob harbor rose up to the house. Around the turn of the century a new railroad bridge above the neck of the harbor brought noise and steamy smoke. However, the scene was still very picturesque.

The Holleys added a multiwindowed enlargement to the long room at the back which added a lot more light and space and an open view of the gardens. Guests often sat there to relax and work. When Willa Cather came here her bedroom and working room was the present formal dining room.

According to records, the house dates back to an old saltbox built in 1732; however, the rare Jacobean fireplaces with rounded back corners and herringbone patterns in the brick indicate that parts were built before 1700. The original house had a parlor on the south and a keeping room, or informal family sitting room, on the north, with the front entrance between them. That original entrance has an intricately carved Queen Anne staircase behind it. In addition, there was a small borning room where the mother of the family stayed during childbirth and confinement, and a lean-to across the back which led to the kitchen and pantry. Upstairs were two bedrooms and a small garret.

Hadlyme

Gillette Castle (NW of town overlooking Connecticut River. Open Memorial Day-2nd Mon. in Oct., daily 11 A.M.-5 P.M.; closed rest of yr. Adm. charged. Picnicking in surrounding Gillette Castle State Park all year round). This is the fantastic retirement home actor and playwright William Gillette built for himself on a lofty series of peaks overlooking the Connecticut River valley. It was not an easy spot on which to build, with its heavily wooded forests inclining down to the river, and he had to construct a tramway near the Hadlyme ferry just west of the site in order to have the material sent up. All in all, it took five years to fashion the medieval Rhenish castle of Southern white oak and native stone from his own architectural plans.

William Gillette grew up near Nook Farm in Hartford (see entry) a generation after Harriet Beecher Stowe and Mark Twain lived there. He was a direct descendant of Thomas Hooker, one of the founders of the city of Hartford, and his family was one of the first to build a house on the tract known as Nook Farm. From childhood Gillette was interested in the theater, much to the dismay of his family, who encouraged him to pursue the more traditional liberal arts. He later became an accomplished playwright and famous actor, most well known for his portrayal of Sherlock Holmes. During his lifetime Gillette wrote ten original plays, one novel, and the adaptation of Arthur Conan Doyle's *Sherlock Holmes* which made him famous.

Each room of the castle is filled with inventions of his own, all constructed to serve a functional purpose. Thick oak doors have huge locks which he designed. Almost all the furniture is built into the raffia-covered walls. Even the electric light fixtures are embellished with bits of colored glass he had collected. One outstanding example of his innovations is the large desk in his study. Its chair is set on tracks so that he could move easily in several directions. The interior trim in each room is hand-hewn from oak according to the minute specifications he dictated.

Upstairs are exhibits relating to Sherlock Holmes and Gillette's theater years. The servants' bedroom has been made into an exact re-creation of Holmes's residence at 221B Baker Street. Other rooms include displays of Gillette's personal possessions, with playbills and magazine articles about his productions, pictures of his family home at Nook Farm, many sketches and notes he used in planning the castle, paintings by local artists, and scrapbooks from his theater years. Ironically, his own bedroom on the second floor is small and drab with a plain metal bed.

After his death in 1937, the castle and 122 acres of forest which surround it were given to the Connecticut State Park and Forest Commission and the entire property became Gillette Castle State Park. William Gillette is buried in the Hooker family plot in Farmington, a small town just southwest of Hartford.

Hartford

Nook Farm (Farmington Ave. and Forest St. **Mark Twain House, Harriet Beecher Stowe House, Memorial Library.** Guided tours start at Visitors' Center. Open all year. June 1-Aug., tours daily 10 A.M.-4:30 P.M.; Sept.-May, Tues.-Sat., 9:30 A.M.-4 P.M.; Sun. 1-4 P.M. Closed Mon. Adm. charged). Nook Farm was home to both Mark Twain and Harriet Beecher Stowe during the nineteenth century. Their houses stand across the green from each other on a city block which was once part of a 140-acre tract of stately Victorian homes.

Among other residents were Charles Dudley Warner, humorous essayist and travel writer who coauthored the widely read novel *The Gilded Age* with Twain and became an editor for the Hartford *Courant;* his wife Susan, a leading patron of the arts; Isabella Beecher Hooker, Mrs. Stowe's half sister, a leading writer for the Women's Suffrage Movement; and her husband, who built the first house on Nook Farm. Their nephew, William Gillette (see Hadlyme, Connecticut), who at one time lived in an old farmhouse at the northwest corner of Forest and Hawthorne Streets, was the famous actor and playwright known for his portrayal of Sherlock Holmes. Mrs. Stowe's husband, a retired professor of theology, was also the author of a definitive history of the Bible. They met frequently with each other over tea and at dinner parties for fervent discussions of the abolitionist movement, women's suffrage, and other issues. Often they were joined by members of the Boston literary circle such as William Dean Howells and Oliver Wendell Holmes, or by editors and publishers from New York.

The **Mark Twain House,** where a number of literary gatherings took place, is a meticulously restored Victorian mansion with nineteen rooms, eighteen fireplaces, and a porch built in the shape of a Mississippi riverboat. Mark Twain and his wife moved to Hartford from Buffalo, New York, after he had come here to discuss *The Innocents Abroad* with Elisha Bliss, president of the American Publishing Company, and liked the city so much that he decided to stay. He then commissioned architect Edward Tuckerman Potter to design the house and Louis Tiffany & Company, interior designers, to develop a daring blend of American, Oriental, Turkish, and Indian styles. In addition to Twain, his wife Olivia, and their three daughters, there were seven servants, three collies, and a number of cats.

Each room reflects Twain's ebullient personality. In the spacious entranceway he had the typically dark woodwork stenciled with light stripes. Where he did not have the walls highly carved, he covered them with elaborate wallpaper. The dining room paper, for example, is stenciled pink and silver. In addition many pieces of heavy Victorian furniture were hung with decorative covers.

The focal point of the house was the library, which also served as the living room. It has an elaborate fireplace with a gigantic mantel brought from Scotland. On it is carved a quotation from Emerson: "The ornament of a house is in the friends who frequent it," which rather sums up what Twain thought about entertaining. On many evenings Twain sat with the family in the library reading manuscripts and asking for their approval or censure. His daughters often acted out scenes from their father's works in the adjoining solarium while the audience sat on chairs in the library. When they did *The Prince and the Pauper,* the solarium was the palace garden or "princely chamber," as Twain called it. Just off the library is an elaborate guest room with highly carved furniture where William Dean Howells and others stayed when they came to visit. It also served as the green room during family plays and as Mrs. Clemens's wrapping room during the holiday season. Many dinner parties for the literary set were held in the nearby formal dining room.

Twain's study, also known as the billiards room, is on the top floor of the house. Here he came each day after a late breakfast downstairs and worked until just before dinnertime. His large desk and typewriter were placed at one end of the room facing away from the windows so that he could see only the wall and his books and was thus able to write without any distraction. Against another wall are his "pigeonholes," a cabinet where he stored everything from dirty boots to uncompleted manuscripts. In fact, the manuscript of *The Adventures of Huckleberry Finn* was lost among the rubble there for several months until he managed to find it and finish it. Behind his desk were specially designed marble windows which had been carved to let the light in at just the right angle behind him.

The walls and ceiling of his study are stenciled very appropriately with crossed cues, pipes, billiard balls, and cigar barrels. The huge billiard table takes up much of the room. During his seventeen years here, he wrote a number of books, sketches, and articles, including *The Adventures of Tom Sawyer, The Adventures of Huckleberry Finn, The Prince and the Pauper, Life on the Mississippi, A Tramp Abroad,* and *A Connecticut Yankee in King Arthur's Court.*

At one end is a simply decorated guest room which he had built for visiting artists and writers. According to all reports, it was used rarely since the guest room on the first floor was so much more luxurious.

Twain's bedroom is as garish as his study. In it is the huge bed which he bought in Venice. There are many photos of him propped up writing there during the later years. He and his wife slept facing the headboard so that they could see the elaborate carving. Each bedpost has removable angels which look like flying gargoyles. Twain died in this bed at his home in Redding, Connecticut. Nearby is another guest room and the schoolroom where the Clemens girls were tutored. That room had been Mark Twain's study until the view out the window distracted him so much that he moved to the billiards room on the top floor.

Much of the basement has been converted into a museum. One room has an enormous model of the riverboat *Robert E. Lee* in the center and is dedicated to Mississippi River scenes. There are pictures of the house as it appeared in *Harper's* and other fashionable magazines of the day, and many etchings from *Huckleberry Finn* and other works. Of special note in this exhibit is an original Huck Finn drawing by Edward Windsor Kendall, recently discovered in a private collection. This was used as a frontispiece for the first edition of *The Adventures of Huckleberry Finn* in 1884. Also here are the famous Mark Twain bicycle and the Paige Compositor, the typesetting machine Twain bought hoping to make a fortune. Unfortunately, he lost $300,000 on the venture and was forced to close the house in 1891 and go on a world lecture tour in order to pay his debts. In 1896, soon after the death of their favorite daughter Susie, the family departed for Europe and never returned to Hartford to live. In 1903 they sold the house and auctioned off the furnishings. Twain died on April 21, 1910, in a newer home, Stormfield, which he had built in Redding, Connecticut.

Since 1903 the house has been a boys' school, a warehouse, and an apartment building. After that it became a branch of the Hartford Public Library and had a guest suite as a memorial to Twain. In 1955, after years of thorough research of all Twain material and interviews with his contemporaries, restorers began to remove the paint and other decorations layer by layer. The house was then meticulously restored to its original condition.

The **Harriet Beecher Stowe House** (same hours as Mark Twain House; guided tours from Visitors' Center), referred to as a Victorian cottage when it was built, is a sharp contrast to Twain's. She and her husband came here after he had retired from the Andover Theological Seminary and established a comfortable but simple home. Whereas the Twain House is heavy and embellished, the Stowe House is light, airy, and modestly decorated. Most of her later novels portraying New England characters and village life were written here. It is easy to imagine this house as the setting for those works. With her elder sister, Catherine Beecher, founder of the Women's Seminary in Hartford, Mrs. Stowe wrote *The American Woman's Home,* popular in the nineteenth century for its advanced ideas on home management and decorating. That book and interviews with her niece, who lived in the house until it was restored, enabled the curators to restore the house and gardens as Mrs. Stowe had left them.

The spacious front parlor where the Stowes received visitors and Harriet often painted and wrote is decorated with many original pieces, some of her paintings, and the kinds of plants she kept there. Upstairs are typical middle-class Victorian bedrooms with the added touch of her panel-painting on the furniture. Her husband Calvin wrote his well-known *Origin and History of the Books of the Bible* in his bedroom study. Over the fireplace in that room is a copy of the famous portrait of Mrs. Stowe which is in the National Gallery. In the small dressing room adjoining her bedroom is the night table where she often wrote and kept her papers. Nearby is her collection of powders and pills. Harriet Beecher Stowe is rumored to have been a true nineteenth-century hypochondriac.

Most Americans remember her only for *Uncle Tom's Cabin* (see Litchfield, Connecticut and Brunswick, Maine). However, in all, she wrote more than thirty-two books and numerous articles. Until the last six years of her life when she deteriorated mentally and lived a life of childlike simplicity, she lectured, traveled, and wrote on a regular basis.

The **Nook Farm Research Library,** which combines the collections of the Stowe-Gay Memorial Library and the Mark Twain Memorial Library, carries on the spirit of Nook Farm. With its twelve thousand volumes, four thousand pamphlets, and eighty thousand manuscript items, it is a valuable source for those interested in the lives and works of Nook Farm residents or the wider scope of American culture during the Victorian era. The library's strong points are its manuscripts and its collection of nineteenth-century Black history.

Litchfield

Litchfield Historical Society Museum (on the Green. Open Tues.-Sat.; mid-May-mid-Oct., 11 A.M.-5 P.M.; early Mar.-mid-May, mid-Oct.-Dec. 24, 2-4 P.M. Closed hols. and rest of yr. Free). This museum has material on the town's historic sites. This idyllic New England town, with its many old homes dating back to Revolutionary times, has not changed dramatically since Harriet Beecher Stowe grew up there a century ago.

In the middle of the long rectangular village green across from the historical society a six-foot memorial to the Beecher family has been erected on the former site of the First Congregational Church, where Lyman Beecher, Harriet's father, preached. The Reverend Beecher was, along with Tapping Reeve, who ran the country's first law school, one of the leading citizens of this prestigious community. (**Tapping Reeve House and Law School.** South Street. Open 11-5, Tues.-Sat., 2-5, Sun., May 15-Oct. 15; closed hols. Adm. charged.) Though an isolated village, Litchfield was a center of culture, and in addition to being home to the law school, which trained many of New England's barristers, was also the home of Miss Pierce's School for Girls, a noted nineteenth-century finishing school.

At the **Old Beecher Homestead Site,** one half mile north of town at the corner of Prospect and North streets (State Route 63), a plaque states that Harriet Beecher Stowe and her brother Henry Ward Beecher were born in a house which stood here. After the Beechers left, the house was moved. It is thought to be the gray frame building on the campus of the Forman School on Norfolk Road, which is off to the right several miles north on Route 63.

The original homestead rambled on with a number of slanted

roofs and chimneys, an L-shaped kitchen, a carriage house, and several smaller buildings. Both front rooms downstairs were used as bedrooms and upstairs were four more bedrooms and a third-floor garret. The back of the first floor was divided into a bedroom and dining room. Since Lyman Beecher's salary was not enough to support his family, Mrs. Beecher took in girls from the local Miss Pierce's School as boarders. Then, when Harriet was still very young, her mother was left an annuity by an uncle and they were able to build a gabled wing at one end with a parlor, several more bedrooms for boarders, and a study for Lyman. They were one of the first families in New England to own a Russian stove, a new invention which warmed six rooms at once and kept the house warm at night. Members of the family particularly remembered the homestead for the rats, which they just could not seem to get rid of, and for the howl of the wind which blew through the top floor in winter.

In addition to the six Beecher children there were Mrs. Beecher's sister Aunt Mary Hubbard, an orphaned ward, several boarders, and two servants. Also on the acre of land were the family cow, chickens, pigs, cats, and dogs. Mr. Beecher's mother and sister lived in a house at the back, which was joined to the Beecher house by a garden path and gate. It is thought that Esther Beecher, the sister, a fastidious unmarried lady who detested any sort of confusion or dirt, was the prototype for Miss Ophelia in *Uncle Tom's Cabin.* Though she did not have the most pleasant disposition, the Beecher children were attracted to her because of her knowledge of birds and animals. Harriet also enjoyed discussing literature and philosophy with her, and it was Aunt Esther who introduced her to Lord Byron's poetry, the subject of a famous essay she wrote later in life. Harriet also became friends with Lord Byron's widow.

Harriet portrayed her early days here in *Poganuc People,* considered to be one of her best New England novels. Litchfield is doubly important because one of the most influential novels in American literature, *Uncle Tom's Cabin,* written much later in Brunswick, Maine (see entry), had its beginnings at the Beecher homestead. Antislavery was a constant topic of conversation in the Beecher household. Though Harriet gained her knowledge of the Underground Railroad from visits to Ohio, and her keen perception of plantation life from a visit to Kentucky, many of the details and prototypes of characters for the novel came from the family tales of her Aunt Mary Hubbard, who lived at the parsonage for the last few years of her life, and from her brother Charles, who often wrote from New Orleans. In fact, Simon Legree is based on a cruel plantation owner Charles Beecher had met while traveling on the Mississippi. Aunt Mary had left her husband, an English plantation owner, in Jamaica, because she found his character and the institution of slavery so repulsive. Though she died when Harriet was quite young, her accounts of the cruelties of slavery were kept alive by older family members. It may well have been her determination that caused Harriet and her sister Catherine, who later founded a girls' school in Hartford, to develop an interest in women's suffrage.

New Haven

Yale University's Beinecke Rare Book and Manuscript Library (corner Wall and High sts. Open 8:30-5 Mon.-Fri.; Sat. 1:30-5; Sun. 2-5) has changing exhibits from its collections. Among its holdings are the manuscripts and letters of Stephen Vincent Benét, Langston Hughes, Ezra Pound, Sinclair Lewis, Eugene O'Neill, Edith Wharton, William Carlos Williams, Samuel Clemens (Mark Twain), James Fenimore Cooper, Washington Irving, and Walt Whitman.

New London

Monte Cristo Cottage (325 Pequod Ave. Take Exit 75 from I-95.
Open by appt. Call curator at O'Neill Theater Center, 203-443-5378);
the boyhood home of Eugene O'Neill and the setting for his two
famous plays *Ah, Wilderness* and *Long Day's Journey into Night,*
is being developed as a memorial to O'Neill and as a museum of
theater memorabilia. In O'Neill's time the green clapboard building
was much more isolated and the view from the house was of grass,
rocks, and the ocean. Pequod Avenue had not yet been built and
the front lawn extended down to the sea. As a young child O'Neill
often romped on the front lawn and played on the rocks as he watched
the boats come in and out of the harbor.

The curators are reconstructing the late Victorian living room as
it was in *Long Day's Journey into Night,* his major tragedy, and
the back dining room as it was in *Ah, Wilderness,* his only comedy.
It is ironic that these two works were set in adjoining rooms. Since
O'Neill gave such detailed stage directions it has been possible to
restore these rooms as the sets in his plays. In *Long Day's Journey*
the original rose-colored glass at the top of the living room windows
bathed the room with a rosy glow until the sun moved on and the
trees made the area very dark. Rose-colored glass has been reinserted
in the top of those windows. In the dining room a door has been
put back into a wall which has been reconstructed so that the room
could have its original screen door leading out to a porch which
went around the house. The sun-room is now used for changing
exhibits and the kitchen has been made into a reading room.

Upstairs the small rooms display memorabilia of the New London
stage and other materials from theaters in the area. Though Harvard
and Yale have most of O'Neill's letters and plays, this museum

has been a clearinghouse for O'Neill material from all over the country. Here are original manuscript letters in which O'Neill makes comments on his plays, reviews, friends' comments, and a number of letters of his third wife, Carlotta Monterey O'Neill, and correspondence O'Neill had with other stage personalities. Also here is the Harold Friedlander-Artcraft collection of window cards, souvenir programs, and heralds encompassing segments of Broadway history from 1935 through 1973. Many professional theater artists are represented. Another feature is the Frederick Adler collection of over a thousand film posters from the 1940s, 1950s, and 1960s. This collection is used to help students observe social change as depicted in the film. Then there are also scrapbooks from the New London stage, which was quite a center for the theater early in the century, and a sizable collection of early periodicals and theater and television manuscripts. Many of the scripts have the light cues, cross-outs, blocking, and dialogue changes. Eight theater models built by noted stage designers for ideal vision and acoustics are also on display. The museum is used primarily by students who come to the nearby Eugene O'Neill Theater Center to take a semester in residence studying dramatic arts.

In the small back bedroom on the left, now an exhibition room, Ella O'Neill supposedly secluded herself and took morphine, depressed by the minuscule rooms and unmanageable house. Eugene, during one of his long bouts of illness, is said to have occupied the front bedroom. One can still imagine Eugene's mother floating down the beautiful wooden staircase in a trancelike state as she does in *Long Day's Journey into Night.* Monte Cristo Cottage also seems to appear as the farmhouse in *Desire Under the Elms.* Here O'Neill describes the two enormous elms which brood oppressively on either side of the house. Ella O'Neill often complained about the gloominess of the trees and the house. Another feature of the landscape here is the massive wall of rocks and boulders which extend out into the sea. There is talk of building farmers' walls in that play.

Anyone who knows O'Neill and his plays will feel the sense of despair hanging over the house. Here he spent a good part of the tragic youth he could never escape. Eugene and his brother attended fashionable boarding schools in the winter and came to the cottage for the summers while their father, James O'Neill, an actor made famous by his role in the play *The Count of Monte Cristo,* came home to spend time with his sons and his withdrawn neurotic wife. O'Neill once commented that he had had no youth. *Ah, Wilderness,* written when he was 44, is said to be a nostalgic dream of what he wished his adolescence had been, a dream of parents who spent time together with their children and enjoyed them.

Arthur and Barbara Gelb, in their definitive biography *O'Neill* (Harper & Row), emphasize how heavily he drew on local scenes in his plays. Many of the characters, of course, lived right in New London, and much of his feeling for the town comes out in the character of Richard Miller in *Ah, Wilderness.* In the play, Miller spent lots of time at the Second Tory Club, an informal gathering place where Irishmen got together to drink and discuss books. This practice was looked upon with disdain by the more established members of New London society. Unlike Richard Miller, who had trepidations about entering the brothels on Bradley Street, O'Neill was quite at home in such places, having been introduced early to them by his brother Jamie. O'Neill based some scenes in *The Great God Brown* on one of these brothels.

Another of his favorite hangouts was the Montauk Inn, which was the prototype for the tavern in *Ah, Wilderness* and also the offstage inn for *A Moon for the Misbegotten.* The inn was on the fringe of the fashionable New London area and was frequented by coachmen, farmers, and prostitutes. The character of Bill Hogan, the pig farmer and shrewd Irish clown of *A Moon for the Misbegotten,* was based on John Dolan, one of the inn's regular customers. He was a pig farmer and garbage collector who lived with his family and animals in a cottage he rented from James O'Neill. Eugene was fascinated by this illiterate man, who was always dressed in filthy overalls and delighted the drinkers with his Irish brogue after he became intoxicated. O'Neill patterned a very funny scene in the play between Hogan and a character called T. Stedman Harder (modeled on Edward Stephen Harkness, son of a wealthy family who spent their summers in New London) on a story he had heard at the inn. Harder complains to Hogan that his pigs have been going into the family ice pond and that he did not like the taste of pork in his water during the summer months when they used the ice.

Hogan, in turn, accuses Harder of knocking down his own fences so that the pigs would fall into the pond and catch pneumonia. The same encounter also appears in *Long Day's Journey into Night,* but there it is exposition rather than dialogue, with Shaughnessy as Dolan and Harker as Harkness. Actually, the ice pond belonged to Edward C. Hammond, whose summer estate adjoined Dolan's farm. But, according to the Gelbs, the Standard Oil background of Harder-Harker really belongs to the father of Edward Stephen Harkness, who with John D. Rockefeller was one of the founders of the Standard Oil Company, against which Eugene had a grudge. The Harkness family had a 235-acre formal estate nearby, at the edge of Long Island Sound; the property is now a state park. In another play, *A Touch of the Poet,* he may also have been satirizing Harkness through the character of Harford, a rich Yankee villain.

All this is interesting in light of the O'Neills' social position in New London. They lived in a modest cottage in an unpretentious manner when they actually could have afforded a more comfortable place. Eugene O'Neill always felt that his parents were snubbed by the elite of the town because of father James's shanty-Irish background and his career as a road actor. His feelings about wealthy New London families come out again through the Chatfields (in reality the Chappells, a family he especially held in disdain) in *Long Day's Journey into Night.* According to the Gelbs, one of the younger members of the Chappell family, after apologizing for the narrow-mindedness of her relatives during the early part of the century, said that the O'Neills were considered shanty-Irish and one couldn't think of them as more than the servant class. Eugene must have felt this deeply, for even in one of his last plays, *A Touch of the Poet,* he wrote fiercely of how the ambitious but defeated Cornelius Melody hated the Yankees who snubbed him.

The **Eugene O'Neill Memorial Theater Center** (305 Great Neck Rd., Waterford. Visitors welcome) outside New London, is open on a year-round basis as a center for theater study. In addition to its regular summer theater series, it is the home of the National Theater of the Deaf, the National Playwrights' Conference, the National Critics' Institute, the National Puppeteers, and the National Theater Institute, which offers a semester of theater study.

Stratford

The American Shakespeare Theatre (1850 Elm St.; Conn. Tpke. Exits 31, 32; Merritt Pkwy. Exit 53. Open for performances June-Labor Day), set on eleven acres of lawns and gardens overlooking Long Island Sound, is modeled after the original Globe Theatre in London. Before performances troubadours stroll around the grounds. Each four-play repertory season includes at least two Shakespearean plays as well as other classical and modern drama. In addition to the sculpture, paintings, and photographs in the lobby, there is a theater museum (open before performances and during intermission) which has displays of costumes, photographs, and designs from previous productions.

West Hartford

Noah Webster Birthplace (227 South Main St., one block N of Exit 41 on State Route 84. Open Thurs. 10-4; Tues. and Sun. 1-4. Adm. charged). Once part of a 120-acre farm, the house has been restored as it was when Webster lived there. Inside are a number of exhibits which illustrate the great impact his spellers and dictionary had on American education and language.

Webster's famous *Blue-Backed Speller,* which came out in 1783, was commonplace in American schools and did much to settle and standardize American spelling. While he was writing and promoting his spellers, he was also working on his dictionary. In the 1780s he traveled around the country extensively, giving lectures on the English language and on education. His lectures, published as essays in 1789 in a collection entitled *Dissertations on the English Language,* were full of linguistic patriotism. He felt strongly that the newly independent America should have her own dictionary and textbooks.

Webster began compiling his three dictionaries around 1800 and his lexicographical activities consumed the bulk of his time until his death in 1843. In 1806 he brought out his *Compendious Dictionary of the English Language* and a year later a *Dictionary . . . for the Use of Common Schools.* His large dictionary took years of preparation and he took orders for it as he went about supervising the printing of his spelling and grammar books. In 1812 he moved to Amherst, Massachusetts, where, in addition to founding Amherst College and becoming involved in civic activities, he continued his research. He also began a systematic etymology, but its publication was superseded by that of other nineteenth-century philologists, such as Jacob Grimm and Franz Bopp.

Webster moved back to New Haven in 1822, when he had reached the letter *H,* and stayed there until his death. He finished the manuscript for the dictionary in England, where he had gone to study the nature of the English language and search for a publisher. No one in England would publish it, however, and he had to import type from Germany and have it set in New Haven. When *An American Dictionary of the English Language* came out in 1828, it was immediately recognized as one of the best works so far. It had twelve thousand more words than Johnson's dictionary, and the definitions and analyses were considered excellent.

DELAWARE

Dover

The **John Dickinson Mansion** (5 mi. SE on US 113, E on Kitts-Hummock Rd. Open 10-5, Tues.-Sat.; 1-5 Sun. Closed major hols. Adm. charged) is Delaware's literary shrine. Popularly known as the "penman of the Revolution," Dickinson came to Dover in 1740 at the age of eight when his father built the brick house on a thirteen-hundred-acre tract. Though the younger Dickinson did not live here after he went off to read law and hold public office in Philadelphia, he often came back to check on the estate.

At the Stamp Act Congress in 1765, Dickinson drafted the Declaration of Rights and Grievances, and during the next decade was responsible for writing many of the important American protest documents. His most famous pamphlets were *Letters from a Farmer in Pennsylvania,* which reflected a logical interpretation of the Townshend Acts. He was known for his moderate views on relations between England and the Colonies; he recognized the right of Parliament to regulate trade by levying duties, but denied its right to tax the Colonies without the consent of their Assemblies. In 1775 he was a representative to the Second Continental Congress, but in 1776 he refused to sign the Declaration of Independence since he felt it was premature. However, once the Declaration was signed, he became very active in government and in 1777 drafted the Articles of Confederation. Later on, he was the chief executive of Pennsylvania.

The brick house with white shutters is set back a few hundred feet from the road and surrounded by open fields of corn and grain with a few forests in the distance. In 1804 a disastrous fire left the mansion in ruins, and as Dickinson rebuilt it, he did the inside in a rather plain manner, since from then on it was to be used by tenants. In 1952 the mansion was restored to its condition before the fire and decorated with furniture from the period of the Dickinsons' stay here. Downstairs, behind the small library, is a parlor and formal dining room with some original Dickinson dishes. Peale's portrait of Dickinson hangs on the wall here.

In the basement are the kitchen and spacious larder which have been made into an exhibit room, with displays related to the restoration of the house and other memorabilia of the period. On the right wall is an original letter from Dickinson to a John Cook of Philadelphia, dated November 4, 1782, in which Dickinson turned over his authority as President (or Governor) of Delaware to Cook, Speaker of the Assembly.

At the top of the large open stairway on the second floor is a small study with one of the few original pieces in the house—a desk that belonged to John Dickinson. How much he used it or what he wrote on it is not known. In this room the young John was tutored by a young Irishman, William Killen, later Chief Justice and first Chancellor of Delaware. To the left in the large master bedroom is the cradle in which Dickinson was rocked, as well as a number of personal items: his straight razor, cuff links, and ink bottle. The only other Dickinson possession in the house is the clock in the downstairs parlor.

MAINE

Brunswick

Stowe House (63 Federal St. Now an inn), where Harriet Beecher Stowe penned *Uncle Tom's Cabin,* is typical of the Maine Colonial homes which had a narrow ell trailing to stables at the rear. Though almost all of the old part of the house has been renovated as a tavern and restaurant called Harriet's Place, the imported fireplace and a few wooden pegged antiques remain. It is still possible to eat dinner in front of the hearth in the old Stowe dining room. Inside the side foyer are wall-sized passages from Mrs. Stowe's letters describing the bitter cold winter during which she wrote *Uncle Tom's Cabin.* At times the children had to leave the dinner table and stand by the fire to warm their hands so that they could continue eating. Henry Wadsworth Longfellow also lived here for a time while he was at Bowdoin College, and the desk he used is still in his room. His fellow classmates Nathaniel Hawthorne and Franklin Pierce often came to visit.

The Stowes arrived in Brunswick in the summer of 1850 from Cincinnati, where Calvin Stowe had been professor at Park Seminary;

Stowe came here to take a similar post at Bowdoin. The family was in desperate financial straits, so much so that there was almost no help to run the respectable nineteenth-century professor's household and Harriet opened a school in the front room of the house to make ends meet. During their stay here she was also to think out and write *Uncle Tom's Cabin,* provide a stimulating environment for her older children, and care for her youngest son, who later became her biographer. That last baby was born in July, and, after having spent her convalescence rereading Sir Walter Scott's novels to her older children, she began the school, and in addition, did panel-painting on furniture for many families in Brunswick.

In 1850 Congress passed the Fugitive Slave Act and the press made much of any slaves who had fled to the north. The time was ripe for the novel that had been brewing in her head for many months. In a letter to her sister she remarked that as soon as her infant son began sleeping more at night she would have the stamina to begin writing. At that point she had no idea that her work would be selling the world over within a year. She had no intentions of writing a political statement but merely needed a vent for her feelings about the outrage of slavery. Mrs. Stowe had been brought up in a New England family which was, like the Whittiers and the Longfellows, fiercely antislavery, and seeds of the novel had been planted in her head early in childhood. In a letter to Frederick Douglass, also written about this time, she talked of her restlessness and described slavery as an "accursed thing."

Pressures to begin the work became more and more intense until one day, several months later, while attending a communion service at the nearby parish church, she suddenly conceived of the death of Uncle Tom. According to her son's reports she became so wrapped up in the story as it came to her that she rushed home, wrote out the story of Uncle Tom's death, and then gathered the children around her to hear the tale. After they encouraged her to go on with the sketch of Uncle Tom and the two slave executioners Sambo and Quimbo, she began writing the novel. Several weeks later, when her husband Calvin returned from lecturing in Cincinnati, she had completed the work but had put it aside, thinking it was too violent. However, he encouraged her to publish it. *Uncle Tom's Cabin* soon appeared serially in the *National Era,* an abolitionist weekly. Soon after, the work was published in book form.

The **First Parish Congregational Church** is located two blocks from the house, next to the Bowdoin College campus. The Stowe family pew, where the vision occurred, is marked with a bronze plaque. At the church are signs to Orr's Island, the setting for her novel *The Pearl of Orr's Island.* Characters of that novel were patterned after some of the parishioners she knew well at the church. British Poet Laureate John Masefield spoke from this pulpit, and in 1875 Longfellow read "Morituri Salutamus," a poem written for the fiftieth anniversary of his graduation from Bowdoin. The Bowdoin College Library has a collection of Hawthorne's letters, and also material from the private libraries of both Longfellow and Hawthorne.

A number of noted literary figures visited the Stowes during the two years they lived in Brunswick. Oliver Wendell Holmes came here, as well as the novelist's famous father, Lyman Beecher, and her brother, Henry Ward Beecher. From here the Stowes moved to North Andover, Massachusetts, where Harriet wrote *Dred,* another antislavery work, and *A Key to Uncle Tom's Cabin.* Glimpses of the small-town life she led here also appear in later novels.

Camden

The **Whitehall Inn** (N of town on US 1) is one of several places associated with poet Edna St. Vincent Millay. The inn has a small Millay parlor, which was dedicated in 1953 during an Edna St. Vincent Millay Week when her dramatic poem *The King's Henchman* was performed at the Camden Opera House. In a corner bookcase are some of her books, an unpublished manuscript, and a facsimile of the original draft of *Renascence.* The innkeeper has also compiled an attractive scrapbook of pictures and articles. On the walls are photos and etchings of her at various stages.

The beginning lines of Edna St. Vincent Millay's long poem *Renascence* describe the view from a nearby hill with its three long mountains, a wood, and a bay. She did her first recital of that poem to an enraptured audience of guests and employees who had come to a summer's end party at the inn. Edna and her sister Norma lived in the nearby coastal town of Rockland with their mother, who supported them by working as a practical nurse. Most sources indicate that both girls had gotten summer jobs at the inn through a friend whose father was active in local politics; however, in a letter written many years later, her sister Norma said that she was the one who worked at the inn and that she had insisted that her shy and re-tiring sister Edna come as a guest to the party.

After winning the prize for the best costume, Edna was begged to recite a song she had written about a circus barker calling people in. When Norma told them about *Renascence* they insisted that she recite "La Joie de Vivre," for which she had received a prize at her high school graduation. A vacationing professor from Cin-cinnati was struck by her brilliance and insisted that she return the next night to recite the longer poem. Soon after, she received a call that one of his wealthy friends wanted to send her to Vassar.

Following her years at college she lived in New York and in Europe, and became one of the most popular writers of her day. Eleven years after her poetry readings at the summer party, she received the Pulitzer Prize for *The Harp-Weaver and Other Poems.* Later on, after she and her husband bought their New York country retreat in Austerlitz (see entry), they came to Camden for a number of summers.

The **Cushing Mansion** (31 Chestnut St.), a typical square-frame two-story house which Millay and her husband owned and often came to before buying Ragged Island, their desolate retreat off the Maine coast, is now in disrepair. Much of the material from the mansion's Millay Room, at one time open to the public, is now at the **Camden Public Library.** There are scrapbooks on her public life, some inti-mate recollections by local residents who knew her, and pictures of her early years.

Mt. Battie, just north of town, has a plaque in her honor atop its 800-foot tower. She often used to climb this hill to see the beauti-ful view of the mountains, woods, and town which inspired much of the lyric poem *Renascence*.

Portland

The **Wadsworth-Longfellow House** (487 Congress St. Open
June-Sept., Mon.-Fri., 9:30-4:30. Closed July 4 and Labor Day.
Adm. charged), the boyhood home of Henry Wadsworth Longfellow,
is tucked in among modern office buildings in the heart of downtown
Portland. Between the front of the house and the sea are rows of
city buildings and a series of beltways. During Longfellow's boyhood
the house stood in the midst of fields, and a dirt road separated the
property from the water. That scene is captured in his famous
poem "My Lost Youth."

The house was built by his maternal grandfather General Peleg
Wadsworth in 1785. When it was completed the Wadsworth-Longfellow House was the grandest residence in Portland. Longfellow
was actually born at a house which stood at the corner of Fore and
Hancock Streets, where his parents had been living temporarily
with an aunt. They moved back to the Wadsworth-Longfellow
House when he was eight months old.

The massive front door leads into the spacious house, elegantly
furnished with original pieces, which had been occupied for one
hundred years by the poet's family. Over the couch in the parlor is
a large portrait of Longfellow when he was a professor at Bowdoin.
The piano here was actually purchased for his Cambridge house when
he married but resembles the original, which was the first spinet in
town. Henry's father, Stephen, one of Portland's leading lawyers,
kept a law office in the front dining room. That is where Henry
studied law for one year before deciding on a career in literature.
At one time Peleg Wadsworth operated a store that was connected
to the dining room by a door on the side. In 1828 the law office
was moved to Exchange Street and the door to the store became
a china closet.

At the rear of the first floor, across the hall from the kitchen, is "Henry's Room" or the "rainy day room." His old schoolmaster's desk sits between the two windows overlooking the old garden. Here Longfellow sat to write his poem "The Rainy Day" in 1841. On the wall is a copy of a draft of a speech by his father, Stephen Longfellow, welcoming General Lafayette to Portland.

The downstairs sitting room is much the same as it was when the poet was growing up and spending time with his family. In the center of the room is a table that he and the other Longfellow children used to sit around to study their lessons. Mrs. Longfellow's sewing table is still there and by one window is Henry's favorite chair.

Upstairs in his mother's bedroom is the cradle in which Henry was rocked and the folding desk he wrote on in his old age. The children's bedroom and nursery, from which there used to be a view of Mt. Washington in the White Mountains, is now decorated as it was when the Longfellow children were growing up. Another of the bedrooms has been decorated as a museum to exhibit some of the gowns, bonnets, and other articles of clothing worn by the family. Here is the black mourning dress which Longfellow's sister wore after his death. There are also a number of showcases containing family possessions. Above the fireplace hangs a portrait of Longfellow as a young man. On the wall is a framed copy of the bill for his delivery. It reads "1807 Feby., for attending on Mrs. Longfellow, $5." Also hung here are his bills at Bowdoin College and bankers' statements on his European expenses.

In Longfellow's bedroom is his old cornhusk bed, the trunk he took on his first trip to Europe in 1828, a small chair he used as a child, and another while a student at Bowdoin College, in which he later wrote "Musings" and "The Lighthouse." He last slept here in 1881 when he made his final visit. From the upstairs is a view of the beautifully terraced gardens which offer respite from the busy city streets.

In addition to those mentioned, Longfellow also wrote the following poems while visiting the house: "The Spirit of Poetry" and "The Burial of Minnesink," in 1825; "Song: When From the Eye of Day" and "Song of the Birds," in 1826; "The Lighthouse," in 1841; and "Changed," in 1858. He described the house vividly in his poem "Lady Wentworth," a retelling of the legend of Martha

Hilton, a plain Portland woman who attracted the wealthy old Governor Wentworth, and married him when she was sixty. A portion of "Hyperion" was also written here.

Longfellow Square, a small plot of land at the intersection of Congress, State, and Pine streets, was designated as a memorial soon after his death. Here is a seven-foot bronze statue by Portland sculptor Franklin Simmons. The heavy classical armchair in which the elderly Longfellow sits is similar to the one in his study in Cambridge (see Cambridge, Massachusetts).

Longfellow drew on a number of Portland scenes in his poetry. He spoke frequently of Portland's park, Deering Oaks, in his time a grove of trees on the outskirts of town, Cape Cottage, south of Portland, and the Portland Headlight, where there is a panoramic view of the shoreline and the small islands he referred to as "Hesperides in the bay." His poem "The Lighthouse" is said to have been written on a visit to the Two Lights on the point of Cape Elizabeth.

In his old age Longfellow himself was a familiar Portland figure. He returned at times to the house and slept in the room he had had as a boy. It is said that passersby used to see him as he sat in the old armchair by the front window. In the museum of the Maine Historical Society, which adjoins the house, is a replica of Longfellow's bust in Westminster Abbey.

Raymond

Nathaniel Hawthorne's Boyhood Home (on Raymond-Cape Rd., off State Route 302. Open June-Aug., Sun. 1-5 and by appt.) is a large white Colonial house with black trim. When Hawthorne first came here with his mother in 1814 this was a heavily wooded area and a dirt road led to the house which stood off in a clearing.

Hawthorne's favorite haunts were within easy walking distance. In the forest just beyond the brook were deer, wild fowl, and bears. There was Legg's Hill, Dingley Bay, and the great flat rock on the edge of nearby Thomas Pond where he stretched out in the warm sun for many hours, fishing for perch and minnow, skipping pebbles across the water, and writing in his notebooks. He also spent many afternoons wandering alone in the woods, shooting hen hawks and partridges, or stripping and bathing alone in the little coves and busy bays of the lake. In winter, he would skate by himself until midnight on the long chains of lakes in the Raymond area.

In later life Hawthorne wrote about how he ran wild here all the time, "fishing all day long or shooting with an old fowling piece," but added that he read any book he could find. After several years, when his uncle brought him back to Salem, Massachusetts (see entry) to prepare for college, he found living in a town quite an adjustment.

Hawthorne's grandfather had bought hundreds of acres here and his uncle, Richard Manning, built two houses, one for himself and the other for his widowed sister, Elizabeth Hawthorne, and her three children. The Manning House, privately owned and not open to the public, still stands several hundred yards to the west on the Raymond-Cape Road. The natives dubbed it "Manning's Folly" when it was built, since the fancy European wallpaper, Belgian windowpanes, four fireplaces on each floor, and massive chimneys were quite unusual for a wilderness area of Maine.

The boyhood home has been drastically altered from the way Hawthorne knew it. During his time it was unpainted and the clearing around it consisted of rough sand and wild grass with a few paths leading over to the small general store, which stood on the site of the present store, and to the carpenter's shop across the street. After the Hawthornes left the house, it became a stagecoach stop and tavern. In 1877 the floor between the first and second story was taken out and the entire building was made into a church. More recently, after a long period of disrepair, it has been restored as a community center and is used for weddings and other receptions.

Aside from a staircase in one corner, some window sashes, and a few pieces of Manning's Belgian glass, little remains of the original interior. On the walls are a few pictures of the area as it was a century ago. A display case of Hawthorne memorabilia holds books, articles, and pictures with Hawthorne associations, and also a piece of the Hawthorne Rock at Thomas Pond, where he went barefoot as a boy and wrote poetry.

South Berwick

The **Sarah Orne Jewett Memorial** (101 Portland St. Open Tues., Thurs., and Sun. 1-5 P.M., mid-June to mid-Sept. Adm. charged), where the Maine regional writer lived from adolescence onward, and **Haggens House** (now the town library) next to it, where she was born and spent her childhood, stand at the main intersection of the village and face the rows of shops which were so much a part of daily life in her novels. Built in the 1780s, the two spacious clapboard houses are among the most elegant buildings in South Berwick. The Memorial in particular, furnished almost as the Jewetts left it, reflects the lifestyle of a literate, well-traveled New England family. Haggens House was built by her grandfather, who had been a sea captain and in later years a shipbuilder and merchant. His house, like the Memorial, was furnished with fine Sheraton and Chippendale pieces from England. It was his legacy which made her financially independent and able to write as she pleased. She also picked up many sea stories from him, and when he retired and opened up a store in Berwick she had another source of Maine life—the old farmers who came in and gathered around the stove.

Miss Jewett's father was the country doctor for the area surrounding South Berwick, a shoemaking village along the Salmon Falls River. Her insight into the everyday lives of the common people came, at least in part, from the traveling she did with him as he rode around the countryside making house calls. While he tended patients, she watched, listened, and often wandered off to talk to other household members, thereby gathering materials for her novels. As the two rode along they also discussed great books. Though

Jane Austen and George Eliot were her personal favorites, Dr. Jewett introduced her to the eighteenth-century English novelists and a number of Russian and French writers. She began writing early, publishing her first essay in *The Atlantic Monthly* at twenty. Her best known works, *A Country Doctor* and *The Country of the Pointed Firs,* describe small-town activities in nineteenth-century Berwick.

Just inside the front entrance is the finely furnished, yet cozy, library which the family used as a sitting room and gathering place for friends. In addition to family portraits, there is a painting of Julia Ward Howe, once a houseguest, and another of Miss Jewett's friend, novelist Annie Fields, whose literary salon on Charles Street in Boston she often visited. Emerson, Longfellow, and Hawthorne were entertained in this room, and it is believed that Henry James, whom Miss Jewett met while on a trip to England, also may have been a guest.

Upstairs Sarah's small dark bedroom is as she left it with the original dark green wallpaper and the large double bed, which takes up most of the room. Scattered about are a number of personal possessions. On her writing desk are slates she used as a schoolgirl, and next to her bed a container of writing implements she kept handy in case of sudden inspiration during the night. Her needlepoint and sewing remain in a pile on the dresser. Prints of scenes she enjoyed when traveling in England and Ireland, where she learned dialect in order to write some Celtic tales, hang on the walls. Just outside her room is a picture of Annie Fields and a painting of George Sand which had been given to her by her friend, Willa Cather.

In the display case lining the spacious upstairs hallway are some small personal possessions and a few minor manuscripts. One is a handwritten copy of her poem "The Queen's Twin" and another a poem of Kipling's which she was quite fond of. In her father's room are letters she wrote to friends.

Miss Jewett often spent part of the morning sitting in a chair by the large window at the front end of the upstairs hallway, looking out onto the village and gathering material for her novels. At that time there were immense gardens in back of the house as well as the stables where she kept horses. She often discussed gardening and other domestic subjects with townspeople she met as she wandered about alone buying feed, hay, and household supplies. During her lifetime she saw the old New England ways changing as the area shifted from shipbuilding to manufacturing. Often she made records of her walks in essays and stories. She wrote a number of stories on the Irish immigrants who were beginning to flock into Maine, and later described life on some of the islands off the coast.

Hamilton House (Vaughan's Lane. Turn off State Route 236 opposite the junction with State Route 91. Open June-Sept., Tues., Thurs., Fri., Sun. 1-5 P.M.), with its projecting dormers and chimneys, stands prominently in the midst of rolling fields overlooking the Quamhegan River. It was the scene of a large part of Miss Jewett's *The Tory Lover.*

Thomaston

Montpelier (1 mi. S on US 1. Open 10-5 daily, May 30-Sept. 10. Adm. charged) is a replica of the elegant retirement home of General Henry Knox, after whom General Pyncheon of Nathaniel Hawthorne's *The House of the Seven Gables* is said to have been partly patterned. Hawthorne visited Knox in August 1837, when the mansion was part of a vast coastal estate. In the preface of the novel Hawthorne said that it "comprised the greater part of what is now known as Waldo County in the State of Maine."

General Knox had received the land from the federal government in appreciation for his years of service as Washington's Commander of Artillery in the American Revolution. He brought his family here in 1795, his career in the military behind him, and after building the mansion lived out the remainder of his life very comfortably. The Knoxes are buried in the local cemetery.

Since Thomaston was a clipper ship town, many elegant pieces often came in from India and China and found their way into the house. In addition to the Knox family furniture scattered about the nineteen rooms are pieces from the empress's palace in Peking, many priceless Oriental rugs, and gifts from such famous persons as the Marquis de Lafayette. One mirror-fronted bookcase is said to have belonged to Marie Antoinette. All over, fireplaces, moldings, and ceilings are elaborately carved.

Local residents were awed by the structure when it was built in 1794, since it was kind of a royal palace on the coast of Maine, then still frontier area. Having a piano was a rarity and the Knoxes had one of the first in the area. Still considered Maine's grandest house, it is especially noted for the unusual "flying" or "butterfly" staircase which forms the central support of the house.

The original building, of which this is an exact replica, was torn down to make way for the Knox-Lincoln Railroad tracks. Much of the furniture was saved, and elaborate architectural drawings for its restoration were made before the demolition. Even the balustrades in the winged staircase and the friezes on the ceilings are exact replicas. In many cases cupboards and mantelpieces were taken from the original house (which stood south of this on the mouth of the river). A few of the outbuildings, including the overseers' homes, have been restored so that mansion visitors can visualize the estate as it was in the earlier part of the nineteenth century when Hawthorne visited here.

A small back room on the second floor has all of General Knox's memorabilia from the battlefield. Perhaps it was that aspect of his personality that attracted Hawthorne. Here are swords, buttons, and other accouterments, and a number of paintings of famous battles of Washington which he, as chief strategist, had planned. Around the house there are also a number of other scenes relating to Washington and the battles.

During those days the area was remote and one could look miles in any direction over the rolling hills to the coast and perhaps see just a few scattered farmhouses. Now Route 1 passes by and there are houses and roadside restaurants not far off. The ocean view is blocked by a cement plant.

MARYLAND

Baltimore

The **Edgar Allan Poe House** (203 North Amity St., between the 900 block of West Lexington and West Saratoga Sts. Open 1-4 Sat. Restored and maintained by the Poe Society of Baltimore. Closed hols. Adm. charged) was home to Poe and his family in the 1830s. Poe had come to Baltimore from New York in 1831 and took shelter in the only home he found available, that of his aunt, Mrs. Clemm, who then lived on nearby Wilks Street. His grandmother, his brother, and Mrs. Clemm's children, Henry and Virginia, were also part of the family. They all lived on the meager pension of the grand-mother, and Mrs. Clemm managed the household. After being forced to leave their house on Wilks Street, the family rented this tiny house, then part of a duplex, and lived here until Grandmother Poe died in July 1835. At that time Poe, Mrs. Clemm, and her daughter left Baltimore for Richmond, Virginia, where Poe married his thirteen-year-old cousin Virginia and also received national recognition for his work on the *Southern Literary Messenger.* (The Poe House in Richmond, also open as a museum, displays most of the remaining Poe possessions.)

Poe House is two rooms deep with a dormer attic. In the small front parlor are several portraits of Poe, one above the fireplace and one above the piano. Though the Poes could not have afforded the instrument during their stay here, it is said to be like the piano Poe would have wanted for his bride-to-be Virginia. Here also is a bust of Poe by Herman Terrell, sculpted after a picture painted just before his death. In back is the tiny kitchen-parlor where the family gathered and spent most of their time. It has the same rough-plastered walls and painted woodwork which are found throughout the house. There are tiny cupboards on either side of the small fireplace and one small window. Upstairs are two bedrooms. The front one with the fireplace was probably used by Poe's grandmother and the back bedroom with the large four-poster bed and cradle by Mrs. Clemm and Virginia.

Up a set of treacherous stairs is the tiny attic bedroom and study furnished with a simple rope bed and desk as it appeared during Poe's time. It is thought that he wrote his short stories "Berenice," "Morella," "King Pest," "Shadow—A Parable," "Mystification," and "Hans Pfaal" there. In October 1833 he won a prize of fifty dollars from a Baltimore magazine, *The Baltimore Saturday Visitor,* for his short story "Ms. Found in a Bottle." He actually received the award at the Latrobe House, which still stands on the south side of Mulberry Street between Charles and Cathedral streets. The story was probably written at the Poe house on Wilks Street. Other famous works written at the Wilks Street house were "A Tale of Jerusalem" and "A Descent into the Maelstrom."

Western Burying Ground or Westminster Presbyterian Cemetery (S of the Poe House, at the corner of Greene and West Fayette Sts.) is the burial place of the Poes. The **Edgar Allan Poe Monument and Grave** is prominently located at the northwest corner of the graveyard, just inside the tall iron fence. Poe's remains were moved here, along with those of his wife Virginia, and his mother-in-law Mrs. Clemm, from an original grave in back of the church.

In 1849 the city passed an ordinance saying that any cemetery within the city limits would be moved unless there was a church on the premises. Thus the Westminster congregation built its church on top of the Western Burying Ground in 1852. Many of those graves under the church make up the catacombs, which have recently been cleaned and restored. A tour of the catacombs is like a trip through one of Poe's horror stories. One large tomb there, some feel, is the one described in his story "The Premature Burial." It is still full of bones. Slaves were secretly brought in through this tomb, which is connected by a tunnel to another tomb outside. Nearby is an eighteen-by-ten-foot pit of bones, a mass grave of two hundred Revolutionary soldiers. It is thought that Poe probably wandered through these catacombs, at that time an open graveyard, by night, and that his gruesome tales were influenced by those walks.

Behind the church several other Poe family members are buried. Next to Poe's original grave is that of his grandfather, David Poe, who was born in Londonderry, Ireland, in 1743, and died in Baltimore on October 17, 1816. In a couple of his stories Poe spoke of the white moss which grows on many of the graves here. The tombs were then often used as sleeping quarters for destitutes of the city, who opened the doors of the tombs and crawled in. Many were locked in and suffocated when the spring locks accidentally shut them inside. Legend has it that students from a nearby medical school would often come and rob the graves.

Poe himself died destitute. He was found in the Little Italy section in a semiconscious state and taken to Washington University Hospital, now the Church Home Hospital, which has a plaque near the spot where he died.

Frederick

The **Barbara Fritchie House** (154 W. Patrick St. Open daily 9-5, Apr.-Dec.; rest of yr. by appt. Closed hols. Adm. charged), built in 1926 on the site of the original, contains relics relating to the tale of Barbara Fritchie. Legend has it that when Stonewall Jackson came marching through the center of Frederick with his troops on

September 10, 1862, Barbara Fritchie waved the Union flag from the upstairs window of her small red brick house. John Greenleaf Whittier immortalized that scene in his poem "Barbara Fritchie."

Whittier was not in Frederick on that day. He learned of the incident from a friend, the novelist Mrs. Southworth, who lived near Frederick and told him the story as she had read it in the Washington papers: "When Lee's army occupied Frederick the only Union flag displayed in the city was held from an attic window by Mrs. Barbara Fritchie, a widow lady aged 97 years." Other details he received from friends who had been in Frederick at that time. Mrs. Fritchie died in the house three months later on December 18, 1862, and was buried alongside her husband in the old German Reformed Cemetery.

The poem first appeared in *The Atlantic* in October 1863, was immediately republished by many northern newspapers, and soon became a popular national ballad. When questioned about the authenticity of the event, Whittier's reply was "that there was a Dame Frietchie [there are variant spellings] in Frederick who loved the old flag is not disputed. As for the rest I do not feel responsible. If there was no such occurrence, so much the worse for Frederick City." When one article stated that there was no factual basis at all to Barbara Fritchie, he responded that the poem was written in good faith, and that the story was no invention of his but had appeared in newspapers in Washington and Maryland before the poem was written.

There was then a series of letters arguing the case in the New York and Boston newspapers as well as Washington and Frederick. Feelings were so intense, in fact, that in 1914, after the old German Reformed Cemetery was turned into a park and the Frietchies were transferred to Mt. Olivet Cemetery, many relatives and friends refused to attend the elaborate ceremonies because they felt she "didn't do it." At that time Mrs. Frietchie and her husband were buried in the so-called Frietchie Triangle and a monument was erected in their memory.

Many also argued about the phraseology of the poem, since the "stars and bars" that Whittier mentions might have been those found in the Confederate flag. Also, he describes the flag as a "silken scarf." Yet in a painting done soon after the event, Barbara Fritchie is waving the flag from a pole and one that large would have been made from bunting. One theory is that Mrs. Fritchie possessed two flags, the large one she displayed from her window, and the silk one she held in her hand.

Northerners began to flock to the scene of Whittier's poem as soon as the poem was published, so much so that after the building was razed to widen the river after the flood of 1868, some came to the conclusion that the house had been intentionally torn down. Actually the waters of Carroll Creek alongside the house rose up and washed away a part of it. The following year the remainder of the house was razed in order to widen the creek. One of the canes made from its timbers is in Whittier's study in Amesbury, Massachusetts (see entry).

Mt. Olivet Cemetery (Mt. Olivet Ave.) has a Frietchie Triangle in the southwest section where the graves of Barbara Frietchie and her husband stand in front of a twelve-foot-tall stone on which is inscribed the poem "Barbara Fritchie."

Rockville

F. Scott Fitzgerald's Grave (St. Mary's Cemetery. Adjacent to St. Mary's Church at intersection of E28, W28, and N355) has an interesting history. At his second funeral in the fall of 1975, thirty-five years after his death, Fitzgerald and his wife Zelda were brought to the Fitzgerald family plot in St. Mary's Cemetery for burial with full literary and liturgical honors. When Fitzgerald died in 1940 the bishop had refused him entrance to this cemetery with the excuse that he had not received Holy Communion. Actually it was because the bishop felt Fitzgerald's writing lacked morality.

At his death, Fitzgerald was buried in the nondenominational

Rockville Cemetery with only about two dozen attending his funeral. A large number of those were friends of his daughter Scottie, who had come to the simple Protestant ceremony en route to a party. The undertaker who arranged the service had to call in a Protestant clergyman for no Catholic would do the service. After the ceremony a few of the guests drove to the cemetery in the rain. Later, in 1947, after her untimely death in a fire at a sanatorium where she had been hospitalized for several months, his wife Zelda also was brought to the neglected plot at Rockville Cemetery. The two have now been moved to the middle of St. Mary's with other members of Fitzgerald's family. The simple four-foot-high gravestone reads "Francis Scott Key Fitzgerald, September 24, 1896/December 21, 1940/his wife Zelda Sayre/July 24, 1900/March 10, 1947." On a slab on the ground is a line from *The Great Gatsby:* "So we beat on, boats against the current, borne back ceaselessly into the past."

Fitzgerald had always hoped to be buried here with his family. In a letter to his secretary not long before his death, he said that he and Zelda belonged together in the polite surroundings of St. Mary's and that it would be a happy thought to be buried there. This cemetery was also a setting for a scene in one of his novels. In *Tender Is the Night,* when Dick Diver comes home from Europe to attend his father's funeral, he comments on how reassuring it is to leave him here with all his relatives. He speaks of flowers scattered over the brown earth, and of ancestors with their weather-beaten faces and souls made of new earth in "the forest-heavy darkness of the seventeenth century." Fitzgerald had come to St. Mary's to his father's funeral in 1931, two years before that novel was published, and made it known that he wanted to be buried here.

At his private graveside service in 1975, Fitzgerald was glorified. Those previously undesirable works, *This Side of Paradise* and *The Great Gatsby,* were praised as descriptions of human imperfection. The Archbishop of Washington hailed Fitzgerald as "an artist who was able with his lucid and poetic imagination to portray the struggle between grace and death," and said that his characters were involved in the great drama of seeking God and love.

MASSACHUSETTS

Amesbury

The **John Greenleaf Whittier House** (86 Friend St. Open Tues.-Sat. 10-5. Closed Thanks. and Dec. 25. Adm. charged) was a four-room cottage with a small attic in 1836 when Whittier sold the old homestead in Haverhill (see entry) and came to Amesbury with his mother, sister, and aunt. Gradually additions were made to the house, and it is now one of a number of rambling homes which line the main street of this small town. Whittier left the farm because he found himself frequently away from home with his duties as secretary of the Anti-Slavery Society in New York and editor of the *Pennsylvania Freeman* in Philadelphia. About the time of the move the English philanthropist Joseph Sturge took him on a tour of the United States and gave him the money to expand the cottage by adding the second floor and a two-story ell. It was then that the "garden room," so named because it looked over the garden, was built. The room became Whittier's study. The addition was also financed by Lewis Tappan of New York, the financial backbone of the abolitionist movement. Both men delicately handed the money over in the form of payment for editorial services. Around the house are a number of articles which indicate family sympathies with the antislavery movement.

This "garden room" remains the same as when Whittier left it. There are bookcases along the walls, chairs scattered about, an open stove, and the original wallpaper and carpet. On the walls are portraits of Emerson, Longfellow, Harriet Beecher Stowe, Frederick Douglass, and other friends. In this room he wrote "Snow-Bound," on a desk which is now out in the Manuscript Room. The desk here is the one he bought after the success of that poem. Here too, Whittier entertained the many friends who came to see him. Among a number of personal possessions are several canes, one made of a piece of oak from the cottage of Barbara Fritchie (see Frederick, Maryland), another of wood from his office in Pennsylvania Hall, which was burned by a proslavery mob in 1838. Here also are many pieces of old family furniture and paintings of scenes in the area.

The other rooms of the house also remain as Whittier left them, with a few minor additions. Since Whittier's death an oil painting of him has been hung over the sofa in the modest Victorian parlor. Portraits of the characters of "Snow-Bound" hang in this room. There is also a picture of the Jubilee Singers from Fisk University, who visited Whittier and sang to him in 1879. Also here is a composite of portraits which together make an imaginary scene of William Lloyd Garrison, Harriet Beecher Stowe, and Whittier listening to the story of a fugitive slave. A photograph of the room as it was in 1884 shows that it is relatively unchanged. The dining room, with its original furnishings, except for a few fireplace implements brought from the Haverhill homestead, is as it was when the family dined here. Over the fireplace is an artist's proof of an engraving of Lincoln that Whittier placed here.

The poet's bedroom was the small room above the study. Here are his original bed, stove, and washing utensils. The green velvet lounge chair was given to him by philanthropist George Peabody after Whittier wrote a poem of dedication for the house Peabody had built in Georgetown. On the wall is a portrait of Joshua Coffin, the Newburyport historian who was Whittier's schoolmaster. Coffin was an ardent worker in the Underground Railroad.

The Manuscript Room is to the left of the front door. Here the

Whittier Association has on display books, manuscripts, and pictures connected with his life and work. Near the door is the secretary on which he wrote "Snow-Bound," "The Eternal Goodness," and all the poems of his middle period. In one display case, along with his old Latin dictionary and his mother's Bible, are paintings of Whittier in his early twenties. Also exhibited are his sister Elizabeth's workbox, made from the burned Pennsylvania Hall, the family account books kept by Whittier's father, and eagle feathers from Lake Superior, which inspired one of his poems. In another case are a few of his early and late poems, among them verses written in schoolboy script but never published, tributes written to Lafayette, Alexander of Russia, and a special letter written to Dr. Oliver Wendell Holmes on his eighty-third birthday, a few weeks before Whittier's death. There is also correspondence with William Lloyd Garrison, Charles Sumner, novelist Annie Fields, and other minor writers such as Scottish novelist S. R. Crockett and Lucy Larcom. On the wall are several groups of portraits, one a group of antislavery friends, another of Whittier at various ages. In the upper portion of the desk are many author's copies and early editions of poems written here at Amesbury. A table belonging to Susannah Martin, the character referred to in the poem "The Witch's Daughter," stands between the windows, and on it are her spectacles. Also a small chair, once the property of Captain Valentine Bagley, stands near a framed copy of the original publication of "The Captain's Well."

The Whittier family attended the Amesbury Friends Meeting House, which stands a quarter of a mile farther out of town on the same side of the road. Their seat is now marked by a silver plate. That meeting house was built in 1851 from plans drawn up by Whittier, who had been head of a committee in charge of the building. The meeting house the family attended when they first came to Amesbury stood near the site of Sacred Heart Church across the street.

Behind the house Whittier kept a half-acre garden with flowers and fruit trees. His simple Quaker funeral drew many visitors, and a photograph in the Manuscript Room shows hundreds of people crowded into the shady garden for the services, which took place after he lay for a period under the portraits in the family parlor.

After the services a procession went to the Whittier family plot in the Friends section of the Amesbury Cemetery.

Whittier wrote of many scenes in the hills around the Pownow River, which cuts through the center of Amesbury just east of the house. If you turn right on Main Street from Friend Street and go south toward 495, you'll come in about eight blocks to the Captain's Well of the Whittier poem. At that point, if you turn right onto Haverhill Road (Route 110) you come to Union Cemetery and the Whittier plot there in the Quaker section. Here in a row of nine plain marble tablets, with Whittier's slightly larger than the rest, are all the members of the family commemorated in "Snow-Bound." Many Whittier fans take a walk up the three-hundred-thirty-two-foot Pownow Hill (about a mile north of town), which is celebrated in a number of poems and has a view as far as Maine and the Isles of Shoals off the coast of New Hampshire. At one time there was a park at the top, but the site has been neglected and access to it is somewhat difficult.

Amherst

The **Dickinson Homestead** (280 Main St. Now an Amherst College faculty residence. Tours of Emily Dickinson's room May 1-Oct. 1, Tues. and Fri. at 3:00, 3:45, 4:30. Rest of yr., Tues. same times. Write ahead to Amherst College for appt.) stands several blocks from the center of town behind layers of overgrown trees. There, a century ago, poet Emily Dickinson wrote most of her poems. In her day Amherst was a village of four or five hundred families on the main coaching road from Boston to the West, and was a bustling social and intellectual center of western Massachusetts. As a young woman Emily was known as the "Belle of Amherst," and she often went on drives into the countryside, on picnics, and to dances and teas, and had a number of intense friendships.

That phase ended early, however, and by the age of twenty-one Emily Dickinson was compulsively attached to her home, often declining invitations to visit friends or attend any of the town's activities. As time went on, she would not even accept callers who came to the front door, and stayed in her room whenever visitors were being entertained. After the death of her parents, her only contact with the world was her sister Lavinia, who loved to travel and kept her posted on events. When no one was around, Emily often wandered about the grounds in the white dresses she habitually wore, caring for the gardens, baking bread, and doing household chores; during the last few years she would not even go downstairs.

Emily Dickinson was born in this house, and except during her childhood when the family was forced to sell and move to much more modest dwellings on nearby North Pleasant Street for a time, this was her only home. For a number of years she attended school at Amherst Academy, which was a few blocks away on a site across the street from the present Jones Library (see following entry). After one year away at Mount Holyoke College, she returned to spend the rest of her life at the family homestead.

The formal gardens which Emily knew and tended became overgrown and have been replanted by later tenants, and the outbuildings, though not dilapidated, are not maintained as they were a century ago. Amherst College has decorated the house with wallpaper of light color and classical design rather than the dark brown wood stains and dark flowered wallpaper that were on the walls when the Dickinsons lived there. Aside from the banjo clock in the dining room and one small table in Emily's room, there are no original Dickinson pieces. (The actual furniture from her bedroom—her writing desk and chair, her bureau with her personal jewelry, as well as her piano and other family possessions—are at Harvard University's Houghton Library, where they are lined up together in a dark room.)

The curators in Amherst, however, have re-created this room as the scene of Emily Dickinson's imaginative life and work. Attention has been paid to small details such as the straw matting on the floor and the thin curtains which let the light of Amherst through and gave her a full view of "the world passing by." Her poems speak of the world she knew from this upstairs room. On her little writing table between the two front windows she watched the world go by and penned those keen perceptions into the nearly two thousand poems which her sister Lavinia discovered arranged in neatly tied packages in her desk after she died. Her sister was aware that Emily was writing poetry but had no idea of her prolificacy. The effect of the room is rather spellbinding when one considers that it was the isolated sanctuary of one of America's foremost poets.

Surrounding her bed are pictures of the men whom, according to some sources, she rarely saw, but with whom she carried on voluminous correspondences. There is the Reverend Charles Wadsworth of Philadelphia, whom she admired, her father's best friend, Otis Lord, who may have offered her his hand in marriage after he had become a widower, and Thomas Wentworth Higginson, her literary mentor for almost twenty years. Each of her biographers has theories about Emily's relationship with these men. After her death her sister and sister-in-law were known to have thrown out or burned poems and letters which they felt were unfit for anyone to see. Therein lies part of the mystery of Emily Dickinson, which may never be solved.

Across from the bed in this spacious, airy room is her bureau with engravings and daguerreotypes of Thomas Carlyle, Charlotte Brontë, and Elizabeth Barrett Browning, writers whose spirit she admired. Other small objects set about give a personal touch. There is the little chair she used as a child and in the closet one of the white dresses she wore. On the windowsill is a basket like the one she used to lower cookies on a rope to the children in the street. The family cradle in which she was no doubt rocked is on display out in the hallway. Above it on the wall is a map of Amherst done about the time she was born. There were then forty houses.

The **Jones Library** (43 Amity St. Open Mon.-Fri. 9-5:30, Tues.-Thurs. to 9:30, Sat. 10-5; closed hols.) has papers of Emily Dickinson and some manuscripts and memorabilia of Robert Frost on display.

Andover and North Andover

The old New England town of Andover has a number of buildings with literary associations. Most are on the campus of **Phillips Academy** and were originally a part of Andover Theological Seminary, a world-renowned Calvinist stronghold during the nineteenth century. (The buildings can be viewed from the outside but are closed to the public.)

From 1853 to 1864 Harriet Beecher Stowe lived at **80 Bartlett Street** (directly behind Andover Inn) while her husband taught at the seminary. During the summer of 1852, before the Stowe family moved from Brunswick, Maine (see entry) to Andover, Mrs. Stowe came here herself to look over the housing situation. After finding the free house which was available to her husband unsuitable, she spent a considerable part of her royalties from *Uncle Tom's Cabin* renovating the Bartlett Street house, formerly a manual labor shop where theological students made coffins and wheelbarrows. Under her supervision, the ugly shop became a lovely home.

During the renovation the Stowes lived in **Samaritan House** at nearby 6 School Street, where she wrote *A Key to Uncle Tom's Cabin,* a defense of her novel. Once settled in her first-floor study at the Bartlett Street house, she completed *Dred, The Minister's Wooing,* and a number of other works. After the Stowes left Andover the house became the Phillips Inn, and in 1929 it was moved back from the road to 80 Bartlett Street. Though she had lived for a period of time in Maine, and spent most of the latter half of her life in Hartford, Connecticut (see entry), Harriet Beecher Stowe was quite attached to Andover. When she died, she was brought back here to be buried in the **Chapel Cemetery** near her house, where her grave can be seen.

At the **America House** (147 Main St.) Samuel F. Smith composed the national hymn "America" ("My Country 'Tis of Thee") in 1832 after being inspired by an old German song he had been translating. He later wrote that he had a sudden impulse to write a patriotic hymn of his own to the same tune, and in half an hour wrote the popular song.

The **Stuart House** (215 Main St.) was the lifelong home of Professor Moses Stuart, often referred to as the "father of Hebrew literature in America." Here he wrote this country's first Hebrew grammar and set the type for it in an old printing shop a few yards north of the house himself, since at that time no one knew how to set letters in Hebrew. His daughter, Sarah Stuart Robbins, wrote *Old Andover Days,* which describes life in nineteenth-century Andover, when it was the center of Calvinist thought and activity.

Oliver Wendell Holmes lived at **210 Main Street** when he was a student in the class of 1825 at the Academy. Part of his poem "The Schoolboy" describes the "swinging gate, garden plot," and "knocker-garnished door." He read the poem in its entirety at the centennial celebration of Phillips Academy in 1878.

At the **Phelps House** (on Main St.), located next to the Peabody Museum, America's first religious newspaper, *The Boston Recorder,* was founded. The house was the center of New England Calvinism when the seminary was in operation. Here religious scholars met and organized the American Board of Foreign Missions, the American Education Society, and the American Temperance Society.

Parson Barnard House (Osgood St., in the adjoining town of North Andover; open Sun. 1-5. Adm. charged) had long been called Bradstreet House, home of America's first poetess, Anne Bradstreet. That claim has recently been disproved by historians. The house where she lived with her mother and her father, Governor Simon Bradstreet, was destroyed by fire; in fact, its exact location is unknown. Parson Barnard House, however, gives a general idea of how the Bradstreets might have lived.

At the nearby **Phillips Manse** (Osgood St., North Andover), Bishop Phillips Brooks wrote "O Little Town of Bethlehem."

The Berkshires—Pittsfield, Lenox, and Stockbridge

The section of the Berkshires around Pittsfield has been referred to as the American Lake District since so many writers found rural retreats here. In 1849, Herman Melville was at his home in Pittsfield writing *Moby Dick* while Hawthorne was working on *The House of the Seven Gables* in nearby Lenox. Physician-poet Oliver Wendell Holmes lived just up the road from Melville and sometimes attended his neighbor. Later in the century Edith Wharton built her summer country mansion, The Mount, and entertained many noted writers.

Much of the social life of the literary set revolved around the home of novelist and schoolmistress Catharine Maria Sedgwick at her home in Lenox. The crowd was often entertained by actress Fanny Kemble, who read Shakespeare on the piazza of the Sedgwicks' home, and also joined the Sedgwicks and their friends on excursions to Monument Mountain, Perry's Peak, and other places. Among other eminent visitors and summer residents were Harriet Beecher Stowe, Henry Ward Beecher, Matthew Arnold, Jenny Lind, and James Russell Lowell. Henry David Thoreau is remembered for a night he spent at the crude observatory on Mount Greylock in 1846 or 1847. By a flickering fire, he read the newspapers that had been left on the ground by tourists. At one point in the night he discovered mice nibbling at his toes.

Pittsfield

Arrowhead (780 Holmes Rd. Open May-Oct., Mon., Wed.-Sat. 10-5, Sun. from 1 P.M.; Nov.-Apr. daily except Mon. 2-5. Closed Jan. 1, Easter, Thanks., Christmas. Adm. charged), a rambling old square house with a huge chimney, stood in the midst of pastures and hayfields when Herman Melville settled here. The property had once been owned by another member of his family; he renamed it Arrowhead because of all the Indian arrowheads he found on the grounds. There were apple orchards on the south side and meadows sloping down to the Housatonic River on the north. The house, now on the outskirts of Pittsfield, has been restored by the Berkshire Historical Association.

The first room visitors enter, the former family dining room, is filled with Melville memorabilia. In addition to the many pictures of the house at various stages there is a comprehensive genealogy of the Melville family. One painting is of a scar formation on an old oak in Park Square. Supposedly that image inspired the scar on Ahab's cheek. The large chimney here is the chief character in "I and My Chimney," a sketch of domestic life at Arrowhead. The twelve-foot-square chimney, built for the kitchen of the original house, is paneled in pine and surrounded by many cupboards. Melville wrote of how the chimney's gentle heat helped mature and ripen the cordials he kept at its edge, and said that the chair warmed by its side would be a better cure for an invalid than a long season spent in Cuba. Above the fireplace is Melville's inscription, "I and my chimney, smoke together." Melville's neighbors were often welcome in this room, where they could peruse his library and drink the cider he made from his own apple orchard.

The Melville parlor is now a reception room for the Historical Society and another room downstairs has local exhibits. There are plans for restoring the piazza, with its view of Mount Greylock. In the first of *The Piazza Tales,* he said that the house was deficient because it lacked the piazza needed to view the beautiful country on the north side. So he decided that it must have one. He said that even in the cold, he would pace up and down on the piazza as if he were on a sleety deck, weathering Cape Horn, and that in summer it reminded him of the vastness and lonesomeness of the sea. The countryside he viewed from here played a part in his works.

In letters to publishers Melville talked about rising early to feed the animals, and going to his workroom upstairs after breakfast to light the fire and spread his manuscript of *Moby Dick* out on the table. His family worried about his health during that time. He would sit at his desk thinking and writing all day until late afternoon, and then ride into town after dinner for a night of drinking and conversing, only to rise early the next morning to walk and split wood before breakfast. In the study, now referred to as the "Moby Dick Room," is a desk similar to the one on which he wrote *Billy Budd.* The window gave him a full view of Mount Greylock, thought by some to resemble the shape of a giant sperm whale. The rest of the furniture, except for Melville's Gothic-style bookcases containing various collections of his works, is of the period.

The fireplace he used to light each morning has recently been discovered under a wall across the hall from the room and will be restored later when and if the original staircase can be rerouted and the rooms restored to their original proportions. After Melville left Arrowhead, the stairs were relocated and a dividing wall was put up to create a hallway.

The painting above the desk in the study belonged to Melville's great-grandfather and was hanging in the house when he came. Melville had explored all sides of Greylock range and in *Pierre* his thorough knowledge of it is revealed. He was especially intrigued by the various large rock formations he saw there. Melville's nearby bedroom is also furnished in the period.

After *Moby Dick* he wrote *Pierre,* partly at the urging of Sophia Hawthorne, who asked for a feminine story without the savagery of *Moby Dick. Pierre* was set partly in the Berkshires and partly in Lansingburgh, New York (see entry under Troy). When economic necessity forced him to turn to short novels and stories which would please the public, he took as his subject the daily life in the Berkshires, writing "I and My Chimney," *The Piazza Tales,* his idylls of the Berkshire hills, and a novel, *Israel Potter.*

Herman Melville first came to the Berkshires from New York in 1850 in search of a place to write and stayed until 1863. He had been living in Manhattan with his wife and sister, but as the pressures of raising a large family became greater, he took a trip to England to see various publishers, and then headed for Massachusetts. He first came to Broadhall, the old Dutch Colonial house which his widowed aunt kept as a summer hotel. The building later became a boarding home, and since 1899 has been the Pittsfield Country Club. Both the house and its setting were clearly described as Saddle Meadows in his novel *Pierre.* At that time Broadhall and its surrounding farmland bordered on Melville's property, Arrowhead. Nathaniel Hawthorne also stayed at Broadhall for a time, as did Henry Wadsworth Longfellow, whose good friend Charles Sumner, later governor of Massachusetts, convinced the owners to convert part of their spacious cellar into a depot for the Underground Railroad.

During his last years at Arrowhead, Melville was going through a period of financial hardship. He was in ill health, received little income from his writing, and made hardly anything from his lectures. Had it not been for some help from his wife's family he would have been destitute. His major novel, *Moby Dick,* was not a success, and after selling Arrowhead to his brother Allan in 1863, he left to spend the next nineteen years of his life as a minor public servant in New York. His books were only beginning to come back into print when he died in 1891.

Oliver Wendell Holmes's Victorian mansion (now privately owned and not open to the public; ask directions at Arrowhead), originally known as **Canoe Meadows,** was built in 1847 on a twenty-four-thousand-acre tract belonging to his great-grandfather, Colonel Jacob Wendell Holmes. It commands a full view of the Berkshires. Holmes took up residence here for seven summers during the time that Henry Wadsworth Longfellow was summering with the Appleton family on East Street. Though Melville settled at Arrowhead because it seemed such a peaceful place for writing, he also picked that particular house so he could be a neighbor of Holmes.

The exterior of the house has been extensively modernized and

Holmes's piazza has given way to a modern glass porch. Down a rolling lawn to the right is a reflecting pool and grape arbor where he often spent time thinking and reading. A driveway leads up the hill to the house from both sides. The original stone marker for the property, a large rock inscribed with an *H,* has been placed at a point where the driveway goes up to either side of the house.

The legendary meeting of Hawthorne and Melville took place at the home of Stockbridge lawyer, David Dudley Fields, who often entertained literary lions. One day Fields rode up on the train from New York with their editor, Evert Duyckinck, and the two planned the event which would bring Hawthorne and Melville together. David Fields invited Melville, Hawthorne, Duyckinck, Oliver Wendell Holmes, author Annie Fields, and her publisher-husband, James, to his Stockbridge home, **Laurel Cottage,** for a three-hour turkey and roast beef dinner accompanied by ample drinks and wine. After the meal, they all walked up to Monument Mountain and found a shady spot where they read Bryant's poem commemorating the mountain. When a storm broke out, they sought refuge under an overhanging piece of rock and drank champagne which was poured by Dr. Holmes. That day Holmes gave one of his spontaneous lectures on the superiority of the English and was strongly challenged by Melville, who wrote an essay on the subject in the days following.

Hawthorne and Melville liked each other so much that the two began visiting often to read and discuss their writing. Melville came frequently to the Hawthorne cottage (see below) and became a close friend of the Hawthorne family. Julian Hawthorne, Nathaniel's son, remembered Melville as "Mr. Omoo," a friendly man with a shaggy coat and bushy brown beard, who came and gave the children rides in the snow on his huge Newfoundland dog.

They also began writing reviews of each other's works for literary journals. Scholars have speculated how much this period of friendship influenced the novels they were writing at the time—*Moby Dick* and *The House of the Seven Gables.* They also took a number of trips together to such places as Monument Mountain, Mount Greylock, and the Shaker villages. After Hawthorne had read *Moby Dick* and spoken to Melville about it, Melville wrote him that he had "unspeakable security" knowing that Hawthorne had understood it, and further assured him that he would "sit down with him and all the gods in old Rome's Pantheon." *Moby Dick* was later dedicated to Hawthorne.

The **Berkshire Museum** (39 South St., on US 7. Open Tues.-Sat., Mon. in July and Aug., 10 A.M.-5 P.M., Sun from 2 P.M. Closed Jan. 1, July 4, Thanks., and Dec. 25) has the original "one-hoss shay" of Oliver Wendell Holmes's poem "The Deacon's Master-piece" enclosed in a glass case. It was donated to the museum in 1914 by Francis W. Rockwell, who had purchased it from stagecoach operator Amansa Rice. His son, Robert A. Rice, told Mr. Rockwell of the poet's frequent visits to examine the old chaise when he lived in Springfield from 1848 through 1856. The chaise had originally been owned by Samuel A. McKay, a leading Pittsfield citizen in the early 1800s, and Holmes had seen it many times when it was being used by McKay. Old Sturbridge Village (near Sturbridge, Mass.) has a full-size replica of the shay.

Lenox

Hawthorne Cottage (follow signs to Tanglewood Music Festival on State Route 183. House is on Hawthorne Rd. Grounds open daily. Guided tours before festival concerts, July-August) has been built on the foundation of the Red Cottage Hawthorne occupied during his stay in the Berkshires from May 1850 to November 1851. The interior is now a practice studio for musicians.

Hawthorne came here in the summer after leaving his job at the Custom House in Salem where he had worked as a surveyor of the port. Boston banker W. Aspinwall Tappan, owner of the ex-pansive Tappan estate, now the present Tanglewood grounds, offered the Hawthornes use of the cottage for a nominal rent. The Tappans were happy to have the Hawthornes stay here and often gave them rides into town or about the countryside in their carriage. For the first few months Hawthorne found himself relaxing after his tiring job at the Custom House and was invigorated by the outdoor life the Berkshires offered. With his children, Julian and Una, he cultivated orchards, cared for chickens, and enjoyed climbing small mountains and running in the woods. Enchanted by such scenes as Monument Mountain, Taconic Dome, and Stockbridge Bowl, which were so unlike the area around Salem, he called this area Tanglewood and the nearby stream Shadowbrook. The name Tanglewood stuck as his writing became more and more popular.

Melville described the house with its expansive view of Stockbridge Bowl as one of the most beautiful spots of the region and said that Sophia had decorated the interior in excellent taste, with fine art prints from Italy hung in every room. Hawthorne wrote that in early morning he often watched Monument Mountain rise out of the mist which covered the yellow fields of rye and the forests. Once, in the fall, he described Monument Mountain as a headless sphinx wrapped in a rich Persian shawl. In his notebooks he often wrote of the changing seasons as he saw them from his study on the second floor.

However, Hawthorne was not so fond of the cottage and called it a very inconvenient house, perhaps the ugliest he had ever seen. His wife, Sophia, characteristically more optimistic than he, wrote to her mother that the rooms were beautifully arranged and it was rather large and commodious though it looked like a small cottage from the outside. She especially liked the nice yard with an old tumbledown gate leading to the lawn and garden beyond with rose bushes, tiger lilies, raspberries, and syringa. Though fields now press up close to the cottage it is easy to imagine that scene.

Hawthorne had established himself as a writer before he came here. The Berkshires merely enabled him to refresh himself after his exhausting years at the Custom House. After resting for the summer, he wrote *The House of the Seven Gables* during several months of intense writing, between the first autumn frost of 1850 and the middle of January. On January 27, 1851, he trudged through the snow with the manuscript and deposited it at the Lenox post office.

Tanglewood Tales and *A Wonder Book for Boys and Girls* were planned and written in a much more relaxed manner that spring. These nature stories came out of his experiences in the woods and fields as he and his children sailed, fished, gathered flowers, and went for picnics. As they romped around, Hawthorne played the hero who could slither up trees very quickly, make toys out of old pieces of junk, carve figures out of wood, and mold marvelous sculpture out of snow or mud. Here was the man of genius in the tales. It was during that time also that his friendship with Melville became intense, and the two spent a lot of time visiting each other. The following summer he planned out *The Blithedale Romance,* based on his experience at Brook Farm, the famous experiment in communal living in West Roxbury, Massachusetts, which lasted from 1841 to 1847.

Hawthorne, more than any other literary figure who came to the Berkshires during those summers, needed solitude. He was not one for day upon day of scintillating conversation. The Sedgwicks, around whom the social life of the literary Berkshires revolved, often tried to call upon him but he did not respond. He did, however, become friendly with the novelist Catharine Sedgwick, and at her school met artist Harriet Hosmer, whom he described as the budding young sculptress in *The Marble Faun.*

Hawthorne's story "Ethan Brand" is also set in the Berkshire area. In the summer of 1838, he had spent several weeks in North Adams and visited Greylock several times. While there he wrote down details in his notebook as he inspected the limekilns on the slopes, and wandered about the town. At one point he carefully observed a crowd inside a tavern as they looked outside at an old German man whose hairy hands pointed to a diorama he was holding. This to Hawthorne seemed a "hand of destiny." He also recorded the antics of a dog furiously chasing his tail, one part of his body a deadly enemy to the other. These incidents appear in the story.

Toward the end of the summer of 1851, Hawthorne wrote to his publisher that he was tiring of the Berkshires and could not spend another winter there. Fanny Kemble offered the family her house, but he and Sophia decided they had to leave the area and they went eastward to spend the winter with Sophia's relatives, the Horace Manns, in the Boston suburb of West Newton. They then decided to make their home at The Wayside (see Concord).

One cold snowy day in November 1851 the Hawthorne family packed
their belongings and pulled away from Red Cottage in a large farm
wagon. Melville was to miss Hawthorne. In fact, his most creative
period came to a close that fall. There is no record of their correspondence from that time on; however, they did meet six years
later in England.

The Mount (on grounds of Center at Foxhollow. Entrance to
Center on State Route 7, 3½ mi. N of Stockbridge), Edith Wharton's
summer mansion, for many years a dormitory of the Foxhollow
School, is being developed as a country inn.

The rambling Mediterranean-style country mansion with a huge
courtyard at the back and many piazzas on all sides is being restored
to its original condition. Inside, the marble floors, fancy wood
carving, and tapestry remain as if waiting for another turn-of-the-
century summer house party. The beautifully terraced gardens,
which went from the front of the house to Laurel Lake, are now
lawns and wooded areas.

In her autobiographical work *A Backward Glance,* Edith Wharton
said that she and her husband, Teddy Wharton, had sold their house
in Newport, Rhode Island, and built this one here in the Berkshires
because they wanted to escape the "watering-place trivialities and
come to the real country." She spoke of the joy of spending six
or seven months a year among fields and woods of her own at The
Mount. The Whartons would come here in the fall and stay until
the cold frost made Manhattan more appealing. Then they would
leave for a round of busy winter traveling or living at their house
at 885 Park Avenue.

When Edith Wharton came to the Berkshires she was well known
for her fiction both here and abroad. Each day she devoted the
morning to writing and then spent the afternoon gardening, entertaining, and engaging in Lenox civic activities. She was known as a
warm hostess who managed to keep the large household with its
many servants running very smoothly. At one point she was described as having the glitter of a New York hostess and the intellectual
distinction of a Boston hostess.

Many literary guests came here to enjoy each other's company
at this secluded country house. Among them were Charles Eliot

Norton, Walter Maynard, and Henry James, who was very taken by the area and described each ride out into the countryside as a "bath of beauty." Then, in addition, there were a number of other distinguished scholars, editors, and artists who came for visits at The Mount for a week or even longer. Following the long afternoon rides around the wooded lakes of the region there were often many evenings of poetry readings and discussions. Henry James is remembered for his recitation of Whitman's *Leaves of Grass* as a house party sat out on one of the front piazzas one balmy summer night. He often wrote of how he was indebted to Edith Wharton for her warm hospitality and the opportunity to explore New England on the many rides they took. Some of those trips later became part of James's *The American Scene*. As they rode around the countryside together, Edith often discussed the sordidness of life she imagined in the poor farmhouses, and compared the violence and incest she imagined there with the conditions Charles Dickens described in his novels. On these excursions she probably gathered material for her New England novels *Ethan Frome* and *Summer*. It is amazing that the author of *Ethan Frome,* with its stark, naturalistic, rustic portrayal of New England Puritanism, summered and entertained amid the elegance and luxury of The Mount. The scenes and material she could have gotten from any of the farms in the area, though some feel that Starkfield was Plainfield, where she and some of her guests once spent the night after a car breakdown.

The actual sledding accident of *Ethan Frome* took place in Lenox at the bottom of Courthouse Hill, which starts just south of the Curtis Hotel at the center of town. The exact spot is the corner of Stockbridge Road and Hawthorne Street. **Number 48,** the low farmhouse with black shutters, now in a modern residential section, is the house the people were taken into after the accident. The event was well known in the area and Edith Wharton would have been well aware of it.

The Mount was generally modeled after Christopher Wren's Belton House in Lincolnshire, with its cupola and walkway on top. It also resembled many of the Italian villas that were springing up as summer places in the Berkshires near the turn of the century. On the ground floor, which leads out into the back courtyard, were an enormous kitchen, a laundry room, and a number of servants' quarters. On the second floor, in addition to living rooms, parlors, and several bedrooms, was Edith Wharton's own suite at the eastern end, with elaborately decorated bedroom, dressing room, and bathroom. Her husband's room was next door and the rest of the house was reserved for guests. Many of them stayed at the other end of the house in a series of rooms which could be reached from the gallery downstairs. In nice weather they could walk up from their rooms onto terraces with awnings to sit and enjoy the view. At the end of the floor was a well-stocked library, which her guests raved about so much. It originally started with floor-length shelves in the living room. Then, when a wing with two more rooms was added on, it became the library. She herself used it only for writing letters.

Adjoining the library was an elegant drawing room with a piano, and beyond that a dining room which could seat twenty. All the rooms still have intricately carved moldings, trim, and marble fireplaces. From this part of the house there was a full view of the beautifully landscaped grounds with tall trees and manicured gardens. Closer to the lake were the stables, several more cottages for year-round help, and a barn.

As soon as the house was finished in the summer of 1904 there was a constant stream of houseguests. The Mount was largely supported by Edith's own money, and though she enjoyed it during the first few years, after she became more and more committed to her writing the entertaining became a burden. As her husband's health declined and he could no longer help manage the estate, they began going there less and less. It was finally sold in 1913 shortly after their divorce.

Stockbridge

The **Jonathan Edwards Monument** (corner of Church and Main Sts.) was erected in his memory by his descendants in 1872. **First Congregational Church** (across street from monument) was built on the site of a smaller church where Edwards preached to the Indians. Near the front entrance is the church's original Indian burying ground, a large mound marked by a stone obelisk. The fire-and-brimstone preacher delivered some of his most famous sermons here.

Mission House (Main and Sergeant Sts. June-Sept., Tues.-Sat., Mon. if hol., 10 A.M.-5 P.M., Sun. 10 A.M.-4 P.M. Oct. by appt. Adm. charged) has Edwards's round writing desk on display. His house stood on the Riggs estate, now the Riggs Psychiatric Institute, farther east near the corner of South and Pine Streets.

The **Red Lion Inn** (on Main St.), across from the Institute, was frequented by Henry Wadsworth Longfellow in the mid-1800s. He stayed there while courting his first wife Fanny Appleton, the daughter of a wealthy Boston merchant who kept a country seat in Pittsfield.

Boston

It would be impossible to list all the sites which have been a part of Boston's literary history. This section is a guide to those places that still stand. Much of the flavor of J. P. Marquand's *The Late George Apley* and Henry James's *The Bostonians* lingers on in this walk through the historic areas around the Common and Beacon Hill. (The Visitor Information Center on Boston Common has maps and brochures.)

The brochure "Literary Boston" has as the starting point of a walking tour the **King's Chapel Burying Ground** (northwest of the Common), which has some of the oldest graves in New England. Most are of local gray slate and the plain Puritan style with winged death's-heads, hourglasses, and crossbones at the top. Nathaniel Hawthorne often walked through during the time he was planning *The Scarlet Letter* and was struck by the small gravestone of Elizabeth Pain on the southern edge of the cemetery. She had been tried for the murder of her child in 1683 and acquitted. Some claim that there is a large *A* emerging at the upper left corner of the gravestone. Hawthorne makes reference to a similar stone at the end of the novel when Hester casts her sad eyes downward at the stone and imagines an angel's writing.

The **Parker House** (just southwest of King's Chapel) was the scene of literary activity in the last century. Here the brash young Ohio writer William Dean Howells came to dinner and met with James Russell Lowell, Oliver Wendell Holmes, and James T. Fields, the gifted editor of *The Atlantic Monthly,* whom Howells was to succeed. The Saturday Club, whose members included Ralph Waldo Emerson, Holmes, Lowell, Richard Henry Dana, and Nathaniel Hawthorne, met at Parker House. Willa Cather lived here for a year and often entertained Sarah Orne Jewett and James T. Fields's wife, the novelist Annie Fields, who was well known for the literary salon at her home on Charles Street.

The Old Corner Bookstore (two blocks east at School and Washington Sts.) has been restored to its appearance during the nineteenth century when it was a gathering place for America's leading writers, who came to chat with each other and browse among the tables lined with the latest books by European and American authors. The building now houses the in-town offices of the Boston *Globe*.

Then known as William D. Ticknor and Co., or Ticknor and Fields, the store was run by publishers James T. Fields and William D. Ticknor, who put out the first works of Longfellow, Stowe, Hawthorne, Emerson, Holmes, Thoreau, Whittier, and others. A number of literary friendships were made among the stacks. William Dean Howells met Mark Twain here for the first time. English novelists Charles Dickens and William Makepeace Thackeray also visited when they were in this country. In 1859 Fields began publishing *The Atlantic* in a small back room, and it soon became one of America's leading literary magazines.

Of special interest are a desk which belonged to Oliver Wendell Holmes and a diorama of the store with many of the literary visitors who frequented it. Harriet Beecher Stowe is outside the window looking at Bibles, while Henry Wadsworth Longfellow, a constant visitor, stands near her. At the counter near the door Ralph Waldo Emerson is talking with an ardent admirer, Louisa May Alcott. There are also many other literary figures represented in the model. Several blocks south is the successor of the Ticknor bookstore, also known as the Old Corner Bookstore (50 Bromfield St.).

At the **Old Granary Burying Ground** (Tremont and Bromfield Sts.) are buried Samuel Adams and Robert Treat Paine, both signers of the Declaration of Independence, the parents of Benjamin Franklin, and Mrs Van der Goose, who has gone down in history as Mother Goose.

The renowned Tremont Theater once was located on the site of the present **Tremont Temple** at 18 Tremont Street. There leading actors and lecturers of the day made appearances. Jenny Lind,

Daniel Webster, and Charles Dickens were all on the program at one time or another. Bronson Alcott's progressive Temple School, attended by children of aristocratic Boston families (see Concord and Harvard, Massachusetts) was in the Masonic Temple which stood at the corner of Tremont and Temple Streets.

North of the Common is the beautiful **Beacon Hill** area. According to "Literary Boston," at **Beacon Street Mall** (northeast edge of the Common), Emerson and Whitman walked briskly back and forth as they argued whether or not the sex should be taken out of *Leaves of Grass.* Louisa May Alcott came to the **Bellevue Hotel Apartments** (21 Beacon St.) when she wanted to get away from the domesticity of her Concord home to write. At the **Athenaeum** (10½ Beacon St.), now tucked in among tall buildings, aristocratic Bostonians came to read before the massive public library was built. Next to the **State House** (at the corner of Beacon and Bowdoin Sts.) stood the home of Major Molineux, who inspired Hawthorne's story, "My Kinsman, Major Molineux."

Many of the stately townhouses on Beacon Hill, now all privately owned and not open to the public, were designed by the architect Charles Bullfinch. Four residences still standing are: **No. 8 Chestnut Street,** the home of writer and publisher George Parsons Lathrop and his wife Rose Hawthorne Lathrop, daughter of Nathaniel Hawthorne; Julia Ward Howe's home at **13 Chestnut Street**—she was the author of the "Battle Hymn of the Republic," and called this area the "frozen ocean of Boston life"; **No. 43 Chestnut Street,** the home of Richard Henry Dana, the eminent poet and critic who founded the *North American Review;* and **No. 50 Chestnut Street,** the home of the historian Francis Parkman.

In William Dean Howells's *The Rise of Silas Lapham,* the satiric portrait of a self-made man trying to make his way in proper nineteenth-century Boston, **No. 48 Vernon Street** was the house of the Coreys where the *nouveau riche* paint manufacturer Lapham shocked everyone by getting drunk at the dinner table while he was a guest. Louisa May Alcott lived a few doors down at **No. 10 Vernon Street** after leaving Concord with her ailing father, Bronson Alcott. This was her home from 1885 until her death in 1888, though she actually died in Roxbury. Henry James lived for a time at **No. 102** and wrote the dramatization of *Daisy Miller* there.

Most of the places with literary associations on **Charles Street,**
which runs parallel to the river down at the western end of Beacon
Hill, are no longer standing. At **No. 148** (now demolished) Annie
Fields held a literary salon frequented by many famous nineteenth-
century writers, among them Longfellow, Emerson, Lowell, Mark
Twain, Henry James, and English visitors Thackeray, Dickens,
and Matthew Arnold. Sarah Orne Jewett came here from Maine
for long periods of time to be in the city and in contact with other
writers of her day. It was here that she met Willa Cather, on whom
she was to have a great influence.

The **Charles Street Meeting House** (now a restaurant and
community center, at the corner of Charles and Mt. Vernon Sts.)
was built in 1804 as the Third Baptist Church, since it was close to
the Charles River and convenient for baptism by immersion. Before
the Civil War the church had antislavery speakers like William Lloyd
Garrison, Frederick Douglass, Harriet Tubman, and Sojourner Truth.

West of the Common, Beacon Street continues parallel to Marlborough Street into Back Bay. Julia Ward Howe's house was at
No. 241 Beacon Street. At **No. 293,** near the corner of Beacon
and Exeter Streets, is the red brick house where Dr. Oliver Wendell
Holmes, author of *The Autocrat of the Breakfast Table,* lived from
1871 until his death in 1894. His study was at the rear of the house
and overlooked the Charles River to Cambridge and beyond. It
was later the residence of his son Oliver Wendell Holmes, Justice
of the United States Supreme Court. At **302 Beacon Street** is the
house which Holmes's neighbor, William Dean Howells, bought
just in time for his daughter's debut. Howells often used to write
letters to Holmes rather than wait his turn at the entrance for a visit.
Soon after he moved in, Howells wrote to Henry James that he
considered it a privilege to have been able to buy a house on Beacon
Street. On Marlborough Street there are some more literary associations. Henry Adams lived at **No. 91 Marlborough Street** when
he taught at Harvard. Bordering the Common on the west is the
Public Garden, and at the Arlington Street entrance is the graceful
bridge that appears in several of William Dean Howells's novels.

Brookline

Sevenels (70 Heath St. Privately owned and not open to the public), the large brownstone bought by poet Amy Lowell's father in 1866, was so named either for the seven Lowells living in the house at one time or for the seven ells which make up the house. When Amy Lowell became mistress of Sevenels in 1900 she immediately converted half of her capital into rare books and manuscripts and built over the house. In addition to writing an incredible number of poems and reviews, she became deeply involved in civic affairs, and was responsible for saving and enlarging the Boston Athenaeum from those who wanted to sell it and build another near the Public Garden.

Cambridge

The Longfellow-Craigie House (at Longfellow National Historical Site, 105 Brattle St. Open daily 9-6, July and August; 9-5, Sept.-June. Closed Dec. 25, Jan. 1. Adm. charged) is one of a number of palatial old homes which line each side of Brattle Street north of Harvard Square. Longfellow came here to rent two rooms on the second floor in August 1837 and lived as a boarder for six years until he married and his wife's father bought the house for him as a wedding present. For almost forty-five years Longfellow and his family lived in this gracious mansion, and many writers came to call on him. Nathaniel Hawthorne, James Russell Lowell, Richard Henry Dana, and publisher James T. Fields were frequent guests, along with Ralph Waldo Emerson and Longfellow's closest friend, Charles Sumner. Charles Dickens, who came for a visit while on his lecture tour of the United States, was touched by the warmth of the Longfellows' home life.

The house had quite a history even before Longfellow lived here. It had been built by Tory Colonel John Vassal around 1759 as part of an estate of several hundred acres. After Vassal fled to England during the Revolution the house was confiscated by the state. George Washington and his Marblehead Regiment occupied it from July 1775 to April 1776. Longfellow's study is said to have served as Washington's dining room, and the room over it was his bedroom. According to legend, Mrs. Washington gave a very festive Twelfth Night party in the drawing room. After the war the house passed into the hands of wealthy Andrew Craigie, who built the western wing and enlarged the square northeastern room, adorning it with columns, and making it into a large formal dining room. After Mr. Craigie died his widow took in a number of Harvard men and their wives as lodgers. Longfellow was one of them.

Throughout the rooms are many scenes familiar to readers of Longfellow's poetry. In the left front parlor, one of the many rooms with elaborate black carved woodwork, is the famous portrait of the Longfellow daughters as they appeared coming down the front stairway in his poem "The Children's Hour."

Across the hall is Longfellow's study, where he wrote some of his most famous poems and entertained friends who stopped by. This room is filled with heavy Victorian furniture and many objets d'art. Against the walls are a number of elaborately carved book-cases, and in the middle of the room is the round table he used for working on manuscripts. Nearby is the upright desk at which he stood to write *Evangeline.* Next to the fireplace is the chair made from the wood of the "spreading chestnut tree" which the children of Cambridge gave him for his seventy-second birthday. The tree was cut down when Brattle Street was widened.

In the ornate library and music room to the back of the house he kept many of the more than ten thousand volumes that he owned. That room also served as a ballroom and has a grand piano. Along the walls, in addition to the bookcases, are several paintings of Minnehaha Falls in Minnesota, the scene of *The Song of Hiawatha,* and the busts of many great writers. There is also a replica of the Longfellow bust in Westminster Abbey.

Longfellow wrote most of his tragic poem "The Cross of Snow" in one of the upstairs bedrooms eighteen years after his wife's death. She had been in the library with the two little girls after cutting their hair, and was sealing up locks of it in small packages for mementos. Suddenly a flake of hot sealing wax fell on her light summer dress and set it on fire. Both she and Longfellow suffered severe burns and she died the next morning.

Longfellow lived here on Brattle Street for forty-five years of his life. After almost twenty years of teaching languages and literature at Harvard he resigned and spent the last twenty-five years of his life devoted to his writing, his family, and the many friends who came to converse with him. William Dean Howells, who often visited the house and wrote about it in his *Literary Friends and Acquaintances,* said that it was "fine to meet Longfellow coming down a Cambridge Street" and that the encounter "made you a part of the literary history and set you apart for the moment from the poor and mean."

Behind the house are summer gardens and a carriage house which has exhibits on Longfellow. Across Brattle Street is the Longfellow Memorial, a statue of the poet with a bas-relief of some characters from his poems.

Dexter Pratt's House (56 Brattle St., between Longfellow Park and Harvard Square) is barely discernible under the veranda of the adjoining restaurant which covers it. A plaque on the front, which is perpendicular to the street, explains that it was built by Torrey Hancock about 1811, and in 1823 became the home of Dexter Pratt, the village blacksmith of Longfellow's poem. Pratt's grave is in the Old Town Burying Ground adjoining Christ Church.

Brattle House (42 Brattle St., now a social club) was home to Margaret Fuller, leader of the Transcendentalist movement of the 1840s, during much of her youth and young adulthood. Here she entertained many noted literary figures.

Widener Library (south side of Harvard Square) has in addition to over three million books, the letters and manuscripts of many famous writers. Major holdings include books by Emily Dickinson, Oliver Wendell Holmes, and Henry Wadsworth Longfellow, to name just a few. Exhibits change periodically. **Houghton Library** (SE side of Harvard Square) has a permanent Keats exhibit and a display of Emily Dickinson's furniture on the top floor.

Elmwood (Elmwood Ave., between Brattle St. and Mt. Auburn St. 7 blocks W of Longfellow House. Now a faculty house of Harvard University), the lifelong home of James Russell Lowell, was one of the last Tory row houses on Brattle Street. Lowell grew up in this plain three-story structure, and later brought his wife, the poet Maria White, here when they married. She died at an early age on the same night as one of the Longfellow children was born. Longfellow's poem "The Two Angels" describes the events of that evening. Lowell lost all of his children except one daughter, who lived with him at Elmwood until late in his life. He spent his last years surrounded by books and friends.

For many years Lowell's study was a room upstairs in the garret where he slept as a boy. In winter, when the leaves fell off the trees, he could have a full view of the Charles River and Mount Auburn Cemetery from his window. In that room he wrote "The Vision of Sir Launfal," "Irene," "Prometheus," the first series of *The Biglow Papers,* and pieces for *The Atlantic.* Later on he had a study downstairs in a room with low walls, a fireplace, and windows which looked out on the trees and lawn. His students often came to find him puffing on his pipe as he sat in his favorite chair by the fireplace, books on the shelves and a manuscript in progress on the table. Here he often taught classes in Dante and entertained friends informally. In addition to Longfellow, frequent visitors were Oliver Wendell Holmes and Francis Parkman.

Mount Auburn Cemetery (Mt. Auburn St.), Longfellow's "City of the Dead," is adjacent to Elmwood. Lowell often went there at night for inspiration and described it as one of the most beautiful places on earth. His grave is in the Jackson family plot there. Longfellow is buried under a monument of brown stone. Not far away are the graves of Oliver Wendell Holmes and his wife.

Near the main gate is the sarcophagus of Charles Sumner, the senator who was a friend to many writers. On a slope nearby is a memorial to Margaret Fuller and her husband, who were drowned off the coast of Fire Island.

Cape Cod

Thoreau's walking tour of the Cape, which laid the basis for his lengthy work *Cape Cod,* can be generally retraced by following Route 6 from Eastham to Provincetown and visiting the spots he wrote about. Though sands have shifted and towns have been built up, it is still possible to get the sense of the Cape as he described it. His route started at Eastham, at the southern edge of what is now Cape Cod National Seashore, and followed the oceanside coast around the bend of the Cape. From Eastham, where the Old Windmill he wrote about still stands, he went north through Nauset Light, Wellfleet, Truro, the Highland Light, the Clay Pounds, the giant sand dunes, and up into Provincetown.

Thoreau conveyed the sense of the Cape in his long descriptions of the angry sea dashing its giant waves against the land and foaming up the sand as it runs back out again toward the horizon. At one point he spoke of the breakers as "droves of a thousand wild horses of Neptune, rushing to the shore, their white manes streaming far behind" the kelpweed as it was tossed up like the "tails of seacows sporting in the brine." He spoke in awe many times of the ancient ocean where "man's works are wrecks" and said that the ocean is "landlord of all."

It was the back side, or open Atlantic, that appealed most to Thoreau, perhaps because it was wilder and more desolate than the bay side where settlers tended to build their houses. He described it as a sylvan retreat, with rustling groves of oaks and locusts, scraggy shrubbery, and occasional wild roses or huckleberry bushes which would appear in the sand. He also commented on how the residents caught and killed huge throngs of birds that descended upon them. At the modern summer community of Wellfleet there is a good view of the ocean as Thoreau saw it. Driving along the coast before that point is sometimes unsafe. By following Oceanview Drive in Wellfleet for some time and then turning left on Long Pond Road, it is possible to get a good view of the ocean and then get back on Route 6.

A number of pages are devoted to the vegetation around Wellfleet and the number of small hills and valleys covered with shrubbery which led down to the pure sand plateau known to the sailors as the Table Lands of Eastham. He was also fascinated by the steamers that came into Wellfleet.

Another stop he describes was Truro, where the Pilgrims stopped while looking for a place to settle. When he lodged here at the lighthouse he noticed the peculiar open country with windmills and occasional herds of cows in the distance. He also spoke of the Clay Pounds, on which Highland Light is built. At that time it was a very fertile tract of land with farmers growing unusually good crops of corn, beets, plums, blueberries, and apples. Occasionally he would spend the night with a farmer and catch up on local lore. He was constantly comparing the inhabitants here to Norsemen and those of other earlier cultures.

Thoreau climbed Mt. Ararat, which rises one hundred feet above the ocean, and described the mirages which occur because of the many beautiful forms and colors there. In addition he gave many accounts of the varied species of sea life, the forms of brown algae, the various sea jellies and mosses, and the cranberries and bayberries which he would come across in that area. He gathered a number of these items to take home for making dyes and candles.

Thoreau visited Provincetown before it became a colony for artists and writers and said that with its magnificent harbor and beaches, it was the most completely maritime town he'd ever been in. The sand was so fine there that no one ever wore shoes. He expressed horror that someone had set up shop in an abandoned schoolhouse and was selling sand.

The areas east and north of the town remain relatively open and unspoiled with numerous ponds, marshes, and beaches. These can best be reached by walking from Provincetown beach at the end of Route 6. Thoreau called such scenes with the sand hills covered with beachgrass, berry bushes, and small pines the "furniture of Cape Cod." It was quite a contrast to the woods around his native Concord. He wrote that at Provincetown it was possible to "stand there and put all America behind him. . . ."

The **Provincetown Playhouse** (in Town Hall, Commercial St.) produces at least one play by Eugene O'Neill each summer. The O'Neill Theater Museum (also at Town Hall. Open daily 10-6 and during theater hours, June 15-Sept. 15.) has exhibits and slide shows. The Playhouse has been in the Town Hall since Spring 1977, when fire destroyed the original structure, known also as the Theater on the Wharf. This theater, famous since 1915, was where many of Eugene O'Neill's plays were first produced.

Chicopee Falls

The **Edward Bellamy House** (91-93 Church St. Open by appt. Contact the Edward Bellamy Memorial Assoc., 6 Center St., Chicopee, Mass. 01013), a Greek revival-style structure where Bellamy lived for most of his life and wrote *Looking Backward,* has been restored by the Edward Bellamy Memorial Association and the City of Chicopee as a meeting place for cultural groups and as a research library for local history.

During Bellamy's day the house stood on the elite outskirts of this industrial town. From the front door he could look over the fields across the road and see the red frame factory buildings along the curve of the railway in the valley. These were the factories of

Looking Backward, run by absentee owners from Boston who made their millions by employing groups of incoming Polish, Irish, and Italian immigrants at very low wages.

The house was built by Bellamy's father, the Baptist minister of this town. Though it has had extensions added, most of the original doors, old slate fireplaces, and mantels are still in place. Taped recollections of Bellamy's daughter have been used for the restoration. Downstairs are the meeting rooms and library, while upstairs is a municipal museum. Eventually the garage will become an industrial museum. Long-range plans are to have the entire block declared a historic park, with many of the houses restored as they were one hundred years ago.

Concord

Concord, known as the scene of the first Revolutionary battle, is also one of America's most literary towns. In the nineteenth century it was the seedbed for what Van Wyck Brooks called "the flowering of New England." The flavor of that particular era can be reenacted by touring the houses of the authors who lived and wrote here. Within a square mile are the homes of Henry David Thoreau, Nathaniel Hawthorne, and Bronson Alcott and his daughter Louisa May. The Tourist Information Center (Heywood St., ¼ mi. E of town center, near corner of Lexington St.) has a comprehensive map of the historic and literary spots. Informative and entertaining tours are given at each site.

Emerson House (Cambridge Tpke. at Lexington Rd. Apr.-Oct., Mon.-Sat., 10 A.M.-5 P.M., Sun. from 2 P.M. Last tour ½ hr. before closing. Closed rest of yr. Adm. charged), a large white structure set back from the road, is essentially as it was when Emerson died in 1882. One of his daughters lived here until 1902, and then it was kept by two Concord schoolteachers who were devoted to the Emerson family and continued their tradition of simple housekeeping.

The study, where the "Sage of Concord" held court with the writers and thinkers who gravitated here, is also as Emerson left it, though the original furniture and books have been moved to the Antiquarian Museum (see below) and replaced by exact replicas. Emerson worked here with his manuscripts spread out on the round table and his library close at hand on the nearby walls. To the back is the fireplace he used to warm himself by in winter, and out the front window is a view of the comings and goings of Concord on Cambridge Turnpike. It is easy to imagine him hunched over the round table with his manuscripts, reading in his favorite chair or relaxing with one of his friends. At the west window is the Aeolian harp which figures in the imagery of much of his writing. Emerson said that during the spring and summer breezes mingled with the songs of the birds in the nearby gardens and brought to mind the wild melodious notes of the old bards and minstrels he loved. This is one of the few original pieces in the room.

Thoreau, Hawthorne, and the Alcotts came frequently to sit and chat with Emerson, and he especially encouraged Thoreau in his writing. William Ellery Channing, who at one point lived in a little cottage nearby, often came by himself and at other times brought his wife and her sister Margaret Fuller. Hawthorne once described him as a "great original thinker who had his earthly abode at the opposite extremity of our village" and said that whenever a writer had fancied upon a new thought he came to Emerson "as the finder of a glittering gem hastens to a lapidary." At one point when Thoreau was staying here (and he especially enjoyed Emerson's comfortable home during his time at Walden Pond), Channing found the discussions on Nature and the Oversoul so intense that he began to visit Hawthorne for relief. Among others who made visits here were John Greenleaf Whittier, Henry Wadsworth Longfellow, Henry James, Bret Harte, and Charles Sumner. When Walt Whitman made a trip from New York, Emerson declared that he was one of America's truly great poets even though the rest of the country was making very little of him. Soon after his visit Whitman dedicated his *Leaves of Grass* to Emerson.

As a young girl Louisa May Alcott came for long periods and Emerson recognized that she possessed considerable talent. In a corner is the swordchair where Mr. Lawrence of her *Little Women,* partly patterned after Emerson, used to sit. In the novel he was the gentleman who lived next door and looked after the family. That portrayal characterizes the relationship between the Emersons and the Alcotts.

The living room-sitting room, where guests were often entertained in the evening, is, like the rest of the house, decorated in mid-Victorian taste and reflects the family's lifestyle and Emerson's personality. His green rocker and Mrs. Emerson's red rocker are set in place on either side of the fireplace. On the mantel is a picture of his lifelong friend and correspondent Thomas Carlyle, whom he visited in England, with a signature of Carlyle's Emerson had pasted to it. In this room the Transcendental Club, whose members included Margaret Fuller, Bronson Alcott, and Theodore Parker, met for long discussions. At the rear is the back entrance the family used to get to their carriage quickly. Emerson's hat still hangs on a hook there.

Just inside the back door is the woodbox Thoreau kept filled when he was a houseguest. He came here to stay for two winters while Emerson was away, and built a number of things for the family. He also repaired furniture, pruned trees, and kept the garden. In the nursery is one of the dollhouses he made for the Emersons' daughters. Thoreau and Bronson Alcott together built a summerhouse, which was to have been a secluded study, and presented it to Emerson as a gift. However, it proved to be too damp and he was unable to use it. There is a picture of it in the small downstairs bedroom that served as the family borning room. The little shack was actually more of an Alcott experiment than a Thoreau design. Alcott built it out of rustic branches rather than the customary lumber made from strong tree limbs and hung mosses over the second story. The whole thing was to illustrate the nature of curves. Thoreau, a man of much more practical nature, helped from the outset but declared that it would not work because it was not of straight lines.

All over the house are family portraits of Emerson's wife and daughters, and a few of his first wife, Ellen Tucker, who died of consumption at nineteen, after only a few years of marriage. When he came here in 1835 with his second wife, Lydia Jackson, after having lived in Newton, Boston, and for a time in the Old Manse on the other side of town, he built a new parlor onto the back to complete the typical square design of the house. Later more rooms were added on the second floor and the third-floor attic was converted into a den. In 1872, a fire did so much damage that the family had to move back to the Old Manse for a year while renovations were being made. It was during that time that Emerson made his trip to England to visit with Carlyle.

In a corner of the master bedroom, decorated in various shades of blue, is a copy of the well-known bust of Emerson by Daniel Chester French, who was also the sculptor of the Lincoln Memorial and the Minute Man at Concord Bridge. In the closet are some of Emerson's clothes, including black pulpit gowns he wore on the lecture circuit.

The **Antiquarian Museum** (Lexington Rd. and Cambridge Tpke., across the road from Emerson House. Guided tours 10 A.M.-4:30 P.M.; mid-Mar.-Oct., Mon.-Sat.; rest of yr., Sat.; Sun. all yr. from 2 P.M.; closed Easter. Adm. charged), a beautiful Colonial building set amid stone courtyard and gardens, was built in 1931 as a gallery for art and antiques from the Concord area. The Emerson family gave the land with the stipulation that a fireproof room be built to house the contents of his study. Here in a room on the first floor the furniture can be viewed through protective glass.

Upstairs, in a room exactly the size of the Walden Pond cabin, is Thoreau's hand-hewn furniture: his low cane bed, large desk, walking sticks, and shoes. In the hall outside the door are surveying maps he had done for properties in the area. There is a general plan for a Surette family cemetery, a plan for land in Lincoln, and a survey for a woodlot.

Orchard House (399 Lexington Rd. Apr.-mid-Nov., Mon.-Sat. 10 A.M.-4:30 P.M.; Sun. from 1 P.M.; last tour ½ hr. before closing. Closed rest of yr. Adm. charged. School of Philosophy on grounds), the Alcott family home for twenty-five years, was almost entirely created by philosopher Bronson Alcott, who bought it and rebuilt it, doing most of the reconstruction himself, and reflects the kind of shabby gentility which was the Alcotts' lifestyle. Emerson had persuaded the Alcotts to come to Concord and develop the property after the failure of Fruitlands (see Harvard, Massachusetts) and the progressive Boston Temple School which Alcott ran with Margaret Fuller and Elizabeth Peabody. At first he had suggested that the Alcotts come to live with him in his own house since he realized how difficult it was for Mrs. Alcott and her daughters to get by on what little money Bronson Alcott earned. Despite his brilliant schemes, Bronson Alcott never seemed to have enough for bare necessities, and the family was always borrowing from friends. It was Mrs. Alcott who declined Emerson's offer and decided that the family was to survive on its own.

When he came to Concord, Alcott's treatise on early education and his *Gospels* and *Orphic Sayings* had been published. Here at Orchard House he wrote his *Essays* and *Conversations,* and his daughter Louisa May developed into a successful novelist. It was through her earnings that the family became financially independent. *Little Women* is set in this house and readers of the novel will see many scenes come alive as they tour the house.

Just inside the dining room, the first room through the front entrance, is a large portrait of the aging Louisa May Alcott, done after she had recovered from a long bout with typhoid, which she had contracted while caring for Civil War soldiers in Washington. Around the table here the Alcotts (the model for the Marches of the novel) often spent long hours talking and playing games with neighbors and friends who dropped in. The dining room also served as a stage for the dramatic productions the girls put on behind curtains made of sheets while their audience sat in the adjoining living room.

Meg's wedding in *Little Women* took place in the small living room, now decorated as it was with many original pieces. Louisa May's famous mood pillow is still on the sofa there. If it were pointed up it meant she was in a good frame of mind and ready to talk to anyone in the house. A downward position meant that she should not be disturbed. The Alcott family piano is in the corner and the busts of Socrates and Plato, which Bronson Alcott took everywhere, stand on either side of the fireplace.

Bronson Alcott's downstairs study reflects his innovative and multifaceted personality. On a round table in the corner is one of the inventions, a new type of reader for the blind that he and his friend developed. They had just completed copying one third of *Little Women* by this method when Alcott died. On a nearby chair is the carpetbag he took on his lecture tours. A picture on the wall shows how the study looked in 1875.

At the top of the stairs is a long bedroom and studio which belonged to May, the Alcott daughter who went to London to study art, married the Swiss Edward Nieriker, and lived in Europe until her death at thirty-nine. This was the room the girls used for changing their costumes during dramatic performances downstairs. Next to it was Louisa and Anna's room, where Louisa stayed during her long recuperation from typhoid. In front of the window on the low writing desk are some samples of her manuscripts. Almost all of *Little Women* was written in this room. In the bookcases on the side walls are copies of the thirty-two books she wrote during her lifetime. Nearby is a picture of Emerson, whom she once described as a best friend.

Mrs. Alcott's room, where the girls spent a lot of time, especially later when their mother was not well, is furnished with her belongings. Here are her spinning wheel, sewing equipment, and lap desk. In the side foyer of the house is a large dollhouse, furnished exactly like the house in *Little Women,* with some Victorian bric-a-brac, and Louisa's own copy of the novel. The kitchen to the back has been restored as it was during the Alcott era, and a number of the household inventions Bronson Alcott made are on display. The modern soapstone sink here was a gift to Mrs. Alcott from Louisa May. She bought it with her first royalties from *Little Women.*

Hawthorne, who lived next door at The Wayside for many years, used Orchard House as the home of Robert Hagburn in his story *Septimus Felton.* Along the forested ridge behind the house where Bronson Alcott walked to take in the evening views, Septimus shot the officer Cyril Norton and buried him under the trees. On his grave Septimus sat with Rose Garfield and Sybil Dacy, who came here to die after drinking a fatal draught of poison.

After the Alcotts moved to the Thoreau-Alcott house at 255 Main Street, a Professor Harris, a disciple of Hegel and principal of the Summer School of Philosophy, used Orchard House as a summer place. The **School of Philosophy,** a restored wooden structure with pointed gables and unpainted wooden interior, stands behind the house, and is used for lectures during the summer. Seekers of truth came there to hear Emerson, Alcott, Frank Sanborn, Margaret Fuller, and others. During the last few years of his life, when he wrote little and had become rather senile, Emerson read his essays as he sat in a huge chair to the left of the platform.

The Wayside (Lexington Rd. Open 10 A.M.-5:30 P.M. June-Aug., daily; Apr.-May, Sept.-Oct., Thurs.-Mon. Closed Nov.-Mar. Adm. charged) was the home of the Alcotts for a year while they were renovating Orchard House a few hundred feet to the west, and several years later became the Concord residence of the Hawthornes. When Nathaniel Hawthorne decided to return to Concord after two years in the Berkshires, William Ellery Channing inquired for a house and found that the Alcotts were just about to move out of Hillside, as it was then called. The house attracted the Hawthornes because of its location at the foot of a hill covered with locust trees, young oaks, and elms. They quickly bought the property and settled in during the spring of 1852. But although they felt at home in this house, they were only to be here a year. Hawthorne's old college classmate Franklin Pierce was running for President and asked Hawthorne to write his campaign biography. When Pierce was elected, he offered Hawthorne the consulship at Liverpool and Hawthorne accepted. The following July the family sailed out of Boston Harbor on the Cunard Steamship Niagara.

Originally a small four-room house, The Wayside now rambles in various directions because of the many additions made by different occupants. Alcott attached wings to each end in 1845 by cutting another house in two. He also added the piazzas. When Hawthorne came back to the house in 1860 after serving abroad, he enlarged the two wings, put two spacious apartments at the back, and added the third-floor study with large chimney and many gables at the top. It is thought that he copied the design from the villa in Italy where he had written *The Marble Faun.* After Hawthorne died and his widow left the house, it was occupied by his daughter Rose for a time and then became a school for girls before it was bought by publisher Daniel Lothrop, and his wife, the children's writer Margaret Sidney, author of *The Five Little Peppers* series. The Lothrops made every attempt to keep the house as the Hawthornes left it.

The old recitation room to the right of the entrance was Hawthorne's study during the first period of residence. This is where he wrote his biography of Pierce. It has old plank floors, a heavy-beamed ceiling, and a large fireplace with two windows facing the highway. Here is Hawthorne's red leather easy chair and Rose Hawthorne's firescreen with its quote from *Mosses from an Old Manse*. This was also the model for the study of Septimus Felton. Through the front window Septimus saw the British soldiers passing by. Over the mantel he hung the sword of the officer he had slain, and on the hearth mixed the magic potion which Sybil quaffed. The room across the hall to the left, at first the Hawthorne parlor, was later enlarged to become the library where he read to his family on cold winter evenings. Hawthorne wrote a number of other stories in this house, many of them thought out as he paced back and forth on the hill in back.

A narrow stairway on the second floor leads to Hawthorne's tower study. He came here several hours a day to work and think, and at times put his oak writing desk over the trap door so that he could ensure the seclusion he coveted. In the four years between the completion of the study and his death, Hawthorne wrote one full novel, *Our Old Home,* an autobiographical account of his experiences in England, and began two more, *Dr. Grimshawe's Secret* and *Septimus Felton,* his only book with a local Revolutionary War setting. Near the staircase is the high desk or shelf where he often stood writing, books surrounding him in cases on the wall, and beautiful views available for contemplation no matter what direction he faced. From the front windows he could look over into the valley, and from the back to the forested ridge, which was his favorite walking place.

Outside is a sign pointing to the path Hawthorne took on these walks when he left the house to pace about, thinking out his works in progress. It leads down to a small cleft in the woods between The Wayside and Orchard House, where Rose Garfield, of *Septimus Felton,* supposedly lived in a little house. His wife Sophia called the woods up at the top of the hill the Mount of Vision since Hawthorne climbed up there each day to study and meditate. Neighbors often saw him pacing the footpath hour after hour, his hands folded behind him, his head bent forward.

Hawthorne did not have the great stream of visitors that Emerson did. However, during the years he lived here he received such writers as Henry Wadsworth Longfellow, William Dean Howells, Annie Fields, and his lifelong friend, Franklin Pierce. The Wayside was the only permanent home that Hawthorne ever had. He came here soon after leaving the Red Cottage in Lenox (see Pittsfield, Massachusetts), and returned to it after his years abroad. In the spring of 1864, knowing that death was not far off, he left The Wayside and took a trip into New Hampshire with Franklin Pierce. He died a week or so later at a small hotel in Plymouth.

The **Old Manse** (Monument St. at the Old North Bridge. Open June-Oct. 15, Mon.-Sat. 10 A.M.-4:30 P.M., Sun. from 1 P.M.; mid-Apr.-May, Oct. 16-mid-Nov., Sat., Sun. only. Closed rest of yr. Adm. charged), which Hawthorne and his wife rented for a nominal fee during the first few years of their marriage, is much the same as Hawthorne described it—set back from the road, approached from an avenue of trees, gambrel-roofed, drowsing away its days in perfect indifference to the passage of worldly time.

Two centuries ago, the Reverend William Emerson, Ralph Waldo Emerson's grandfather, stood on the field closest to the North Bridge and urged the minutemen fighting there to flee to the house for safety while his wife and children watched from the bedroom upstairs. The Reverend Emerson, who died a year later en route home from his post as chaplain at Fort Ticonderoga, was the first occupant of the Old Manse. After he died, Mrs. Emerson married Dr. Ezra Ripley, another prominent clergyman who adopted her children. Years later Ralph Waldo Emerson visited his grandfather's home often and, in fact, lived there with his mother from 1834 to 1835, after the death of his first wife, Ellen Tucker. *Nature,* his first book of essays, was written in the upstairs study.

In 1835, Emerson married Lydia Jackson of Plymouth and they moved to the Emerson House on Cambridge Turnpike. Except for the years when the house was rented to Nathaniel and Sophia Hawthorne, the Old Manse has been lived in by members of the Emerson family. In 1939 it was passed into the hands of the Trustees of Reservations in much the same condition as a century before when the two great authors lived there. Its decor is that of a well-to-do minister's home, with dark Victorian wallpaper, antique-brown-finished walls, and the eighteenth-century furniture of its first occupants. Though an Emerson family house, the Manse is remembered more for its association with Hawthorne, since he described it in his *Mosses from an Old Manse,* an account of the years he and Sophia spent there.

Hawthorne wrote that his stay here was a time of "almost idyllic" happiness, a time when he was happy and free of care, and said that he often recollected the solitude of the river, the avenue, the orchard, and especially the Manse itself when the sun glimmered through the willow branches into his study. The tranquil Concord River, which inspired so many of the town's writers, flows behind the house. It is a very narrow stream with lilies and grasses growing along its edge. Emerson spoke of Thoreau as the River God who introduced him to the "shadowy, starlit, moonlit stream." In *A Week on the Concord and Merrimack Rivers* Thoreau described a trip he took with his brother in their handcrafted boat.

That boat was later sold to Hawthorne when he moved to the Old Manse and wanted to take rides up and down the river. During the friendship that the two writers developed that year, Thoreau spent many hours teaching Hawthorne how to steer the cumbersome boat, which he rechristened "Pond Lily." Thoreau also came to skate with Hawthorne, who hobbled along on the ice in a long cloak and marveled at Thoreau's agility as he skipped over the ice like a fawn. As the two spent time skating, taking walks, or rowing along, Thoreau instructed Hawthorne on many aspects of nature. Their friendship more or less ended in the spring of 1843 when Thoreau left for Staten Island to be resident tutor for the family of Ralph Waldo Emerson's brother.

During their stay at the Manse, the Hawthornes spent much of their time in the breakfast room which looked out onto the river. Sophia used the breakfast room as a studio for painting and said she enjoyed working there because she could hear her husband rumbling in his study above. He would throw his scrap papers down the back stairs and she would put them into the fireplace for him. On the side window is some of the etching she did with her diamond ring. She described a storm that she and her baby daughter, Una, saw as they looked out the window one winter day. Upstairs on a window in the study is a dialogue in diamond writing between Nathaniel and Sophia. It reads, "Nath.' Hawthorne. This is his

study; 1843." Sophia had written below, "Inscribed by my husband
at Sunset Apr. 3^d 1843. In the gold light S. A. H. Man's accidents
are God's purposes. Sophia A. Hawthorne 1843-."

Hawthorne worked upstairs alone three or four hours a day.
Next to the fireplace in this small study is the stand-up desk where
he penned all of *Mosses,* did many articles for the *Democratic
Review* and other magazines, and edited a number of works. It is
ironic that in the very room where Emerson wrote *Nature,* which
began the Transcendentalist movement, Hawthorne condemned
the terrible giant "transcendentalist" who was being substituted
for Alexander Pope and Bunyan's allegory. Although Hawthorne
said that this first home of his was heaven to him, he could not
afford to stay here. On either side of the fireplace are portraits
of both writers.

Hawthorne's was the right front bedroom, at times referred to
as the "Saint's Chamber" or "Parson's Room," for the generations
of clergymen who used it. The luxurious daybed he rested on is still
here between the windows. On the wall is a picture of his daughter,
Una. In the front room, known as Emerson's bedroom, is the
stand-up sermon desk where Ezra Ripley stood to write his three-
hour-long sermons each week. Above the fireplace is a chart of the
kings of England which Sarah Alden Bradstreet Ripley, who lived
here after the Hawthornes and ran her own preparatory school,
used to quiz the boys preparing for the Harvard entrance exam.
There is a large portrait of her over the fireplace in the formal parlor
downstairs where the Emerson families did much of their entertaining.

The Hawthornes used the darker, more informal sitting room
on the left. Emerson, Thoreau, William Ellery Channing, Margaret
Fuller, James Russell Lowell, and Hawthorne's college classmate,
Franklin Pierce, all came to visit the Hawthornes and discuss their
views. While they drank sherry and ate they often listened to the
music box that had been left here by Thoreau. During the winter
they gathered around the fire and told ghost stories.

Sophia Hawthorne decorated the house with paintings and put
fruit and flowers around to make everything look lighter. She also
painted beds and chairs with scenes from Greek and Roman myths.
Biographers attribute Hawthorne's happiness here, in part at least,
to her gay spirit. She often danced by the music box in the parlor,
read Shakespeare and Goethe with her husband by an oil lamp, and

encouraged him to take walks along the river and into the fields on
moonlit nights. At times she would go off to visit her family for a
week and Hawthorne would spend his time at the now-demolished
village Athenaeum, since he could not stand to be alone by himself.

The townspeople thought of Hawthorne as a recluse. Between
the house and the battlefields at that time were fields of tall grass,
where Hawthorne kept a garden. Neighbors reported seeing him
clad in dark clothes, hoeing for what seemed like extended periods
of time, and gazing fixedly at the ground. He took his gardening
seriously and in his notebooks spoke of the peas and potatoes he
grew here and of the "unconscionable squash bugs" against which
he had a continual war. He described the calm of the place with its
"near retirement and accessible seclusion," not bleak enough to be
totally isolated yet sufficiently hedged in to make casual intrusion
unlikely.

The atmosphere at the Manse no doubt influenced Hawthorne's
writing. At times, on wet, dark days, he rummaged around in the
twilight of the unfinished garret of the Manse, looking through
piles of old theological works, sermons, and tracts. While he was
there he began to write his dark allegories. The theme of isolation
and its accompanying sense of guilt are very evident in the Owen
Warland of *Mosses,* who was so alienated from his neighbors that
they thought him mad. This period is thought to have laid the basis
for his later stories.

To the right of the house is a dirt path leading down to the **North
Bridge,** where Daniel Chester French's bronze Minute Man marks
the spot of first resistance to the British. On the monument is
Emerson's "Concord Hymn" which celebrates the embattled farmers
who stood here and "fired the shot heard round the world." One
legend says that a young minuteman took an ax from the Manse
woodpile and finished off a British soldier who had not yet died.
This story had a chilling effect on Hawthorne and he related it in
his later romance, *Septimus Felton.* One night when Hawthorne
and William Ellery Channing were rowing under the North Bridge
here, they came upon the body of a young girl who had committed
suicide by throwing herself into the river. The horror he felt as he
took the body from the water comes out in a similar scene at the
end of the tale of Zenobia in *The Blithedale Romance.*

At **Walden Pond State Reservation** (915 Walden St., S of

town. Open all yr., daylight hrs. Two-hundred-acre-park with swimming beach and picnic grounds), a trail marked with white *T's* leads through the woods to the site of Thoreau's cabin across the pond from the entrance. The first quarter of the walk is disheartening since the populated area of the woods is no longer a sylvan retreat. Local fishermen often sit on the edge of the pond blaring their radios and local teenagers wear the path down as they speed by on their motorcycles. However, the natural beauty of the area returns once you pass this section.

The cabin site, discovered in 1945, is marked off by an outline of stones and a chain fence. From here Thoreau would arise each morning and look through the pine trees to the pond about a hundred feet away. In this small area he fit his hand-hewn furniture: the cane bed, the desk, and several chairs, which are on display at the Antiquarian Museum. There are still a few evidences of the chimney foundation at one end.

Nearby is a plaque with a quotation from the beginning of his essay "Where I Lived and What I Lived For." It reads, "I went to the woods to live completely, to front the essential facts of life." In that essay he described the cottage which stood on this site. Materials cost $28.12½. He borrowed Bronson Alcott's ax and cut down some nearby pines for timbers, studs, and rafters. Then he bought a shanty from one of the Irish laborers at the railroad and used that for the boards and some of the furniture. The finished product was ten by fifteen feet, had a shingled roof, plastered walls on the inside, windows on all sides, and a trap door to a storage cellar. Nearby in a bean field he planted potatoes, corn, and other vegetables. Bronson Alcott stopped by at one point to help him build.

Thoreau came here soon after returning from Staten Island where he had been tutoring Emerson's brother's children. In this cabin he wrote most of *Walden* and *A Week on the Concord and Merrimack Rivers*. During his stay here he also went to jail for refusing to pay his poll taxes. Thoreau left Walden in the fall of 1847 when he went to stay with the Emerson family while Emerson went off to Europe. Soon after that a gardener moved the hut to the middle of a bean field and lived in it a number of years. Later it was moved to a farm and used as a toolshed until it finally collapsed.

Emerson, who owned the land, was Thoreau's most frequent

visitor. However, Bronson Alcott, Ellery Channing, and Hawthorne also came at times, and Thoreau often let wanderers come in for the night. Behind the cabin are the railroad tracks he used to walk along when he went to visit his family at their home next to the present Thoreau Lyceum. The clusters of Irish shanties he spoke of in *Walden* were on the farmlands beyond the tracks.

Though Walden Pond has become synonymous with Thoreau, Emerson also came here often for solitude and meditation. His spot was a wooded place on a wild rocky ledge, not far from the site of Thoreau's cabin, where he rowed his boat, played his flute, and wrote in his journal. Most of the material for *Wood Notes* was collected as he sat in a little pine garden where chickadees flitted through the branches. At times he came at night during the full moon to smell the ferns and flowers. He said that here he felt "adjacent to the One, like a king in the woods in a state of elevation shared by all the mystics."

Thoreau Lyceum (156 Belknap St. Mon.-Sat., 10 A.M.-5 P.M., Sun. from 2 P.M. Closed major hols. Free), though largely an art gallery, houses various objects which belonged to Thoreau. It was formed in 1966 by a group of residents who felt there should be a Thoreau center in Concord. On the first floor is one of his desks, a Ricketson bust, original surveying maps, some of his Indian artifacts from the Connecticut River valley, and some old maps he used. On the second floor are changing exhibits based on his varied interests and on other Transcendentalists. There is also a small research library for study and general research. Both Thoreau and Emerson lectured at the original Lyceum and Thoreau acted as secretary for a time.

Under the brush to the left of the building are remnants of the old Thoreau homestead, where his family lived while he was at Walden Pond. The railroad tracks he used to walk along from his cabin are directly behind this lot. In the backyard of the Lyceum is an exact replica of the Walden Pond Cabin, complete with furniture. Over the door is the quotation that Thoreau had carved into the original cabin: "Entertainment for man, but not for beast."

The **Thoreau-Alcott House** (255 Main St.), now privately owned and not open to the public, was home to Henry David Thoreau after his family left their house on Belknap Street. The Alcotts lived here after they left Orchard House. Thoreau planted many of the large trees surrounding the house and erected some of the walls within. In the second story of the extension at the back of the house the family had a small pencil factory. The room to the right of the front entrance served as Thoreau's study and later as the sitting room of the Alcotts. He also had a room in the attic where he kept his collection of Indian artifacts, rocks, and odd pieces of driftwood. The Thoreaus often hid fugitive slaves, and John Brown, the fanatical abolitionist, was often a welcome guest. William Ellery Channing lived in a little house across the street after he left his wife and children. Channing and Thoreau took the journey Thoreau described in *Yankee in Canada.*

The room to the left of the front entrance was Louisa May Alcott's study. There she did her writing and nursed her father after he had suffered his stroke. Mrs. Alcott (Marmee of *Little Women*) died in the house soon after they moved here. It was also the home of "Meg," the mother of *Little Men* and widow of "John Brooke" of the Alcott books. After the Alcotts left, Hawthorne and Emerson sent their children to a school which Frank Sanborn, a friend of many Concord writers and a later occupant of the house, kept in one of the back rooms.

The site of the **Old Jail** (designated by a marker), where Thoreau spent the night for refusing to pay his poll taxes, is on the southwest corner of Monument Square in the center of town. He thought that the government supported slavery and had entered the Mexican War as an excuse to seize more slave territory; therefore, he refused to pay his poll tax, hoping to be put in jail as Bronson Alcott had been and to draw attention to his beliefs. After four years of not paying the taxes he was finally arrested in July, 1846, but spent only one night there since a devoted aunt came over immediately and paid his tax. That experience spurred him on to write his essay "Civil Disobedience."

Sleepy Hollow Cemetery (on Bedford St., State Route 62, NE of town square. Follow signs inside gate to "Authors' Ridge") is now the meeting ground for Concord's great authors, who lie buried on the northeast side of the cemetery. Henry David Thoreau's

simple eight-by-seven-inch gravestone is one of the first at the top
of the hill. He is buried here in the family plot along with his two
sisters, three brothers, and his parents. On the north side of the
path is the Hawthorne family plot, surrounded by a chain fence.
Alongside Hawthorne's grave is a memorial to his wife, Sophia,
and their daughter, Una, who are buried in Kensal Green, London,
where they had gone after his death. On the south side of the path
is the Emerson family plot, also surrounded by a chain fence. An
unusual pointed granite rock marks Emerson's grave. The inscription on it faces away from the path toward the cemetery, and is
easy to miss. Between the Thoreau and Emerson plots, and lying
diagonally across from the Hawthornes', is the Alcott family plot.
Here lie the social reformer, Bronson Alcott, his daughter, the
novelist Louisa May, her sisters, and their mother. William Ellery
Channing is by himself to the north, almost on the precipice of
the ridge.

Hawthorne and his wife took walks here when Sleepy Hollow
was an open area of verdant fields, and they often met Emerson,
Thoreau, Alcott, and Margaret Fuller, who were also taking strolls.
Emerson wrote the dedication when the beautiful park became
a cemetery.

Cummington

The **William Cullen Bryant Homestead** (follow signs from State
Route 9. Open daily except Mon. 2-5 P.M., June 15-Sept. 1 and
weekends until Oct. 15. Adm. charged) is an expansive country
house which lies tucked among the rolling hills of Hampshire County
in western Massachusetts. Bryant, who has been referred to as the
"American Wordsworth," was born about a half mile from the

homestead on Potash Hill Road. A granite monument across from Dawes Cemetery marks the site of the birthplace.

According to one of Bryant's letters, the homestead was built in 1783 by Bryant's grandfather, Ebenezer Snell, one of the area's first settlers. His father, Dr. Peter Bryant, was the physician for the area. Bryant spent his childhood here with his parents and his four brothers and two sisters, and began writing poetry at the age of eight. In a short autobiographical piece he explained that he always had been very advanced for his age and was encouraged to write poetry by his father, who dabbled in verse himself and had an extensive collection of the noted English poets.

At sixteen he wrote "Thanatopsis" as he sat in his small upstairs bedroom. It seems that he had been reading poems on death by several authors and that when he came home after spending time in the woods he conceived the poem. When the prestigious *North American Review* received the poem in 1817 they were at first reluctant to print it since they felt that "no one on this side of the Atlantic is capable of producing such verse."

Bryant left this house when he went to practice law slightly south at Great Barrington, where the climate would be better for his consumption. At that time he described himself as "wasted to a shadow because of a complaint of the lungs," and since his father and sister had died of consumption, he really feared that his years were numbered. As soon as he settled at a local law office his health improved and he became one of the town leaders. He was first appointed one of the tithing men, whose duty it was to keep order in the churches and enforce the observance of the Sabbath. Soon after, he became town clerk and had to keep track of the functioning of the town. It was his responsibility to appoint selectmen, highway surveyors, and bailiffs to mediate small property disputes. For this he received an annual salary of five dollars. Then the governor of Massachusetts made him Justice of the Peace, a post which enabled him to hear and try small cases. At one point he confided to a friend that he was quite bored with those activities and much preferred to spend his time writing. After about five years in Great Barrington, Bryant left for New York, where he pursued writing as a career and later became editor of the New York *Evening Post*.

The homestead in Cummington had been sold by Bryant's parents in 1835, but in 1865, Bryant, who was by that time fairly wealthy, bought it back for his ailing wife. He remodeled it extensively by raising the original house and building a new floor underneath. Many of the thirteen hundred trees he planted still stand on the grounds. Unfortunately, his wife died just before the renovations were completed, and he and his daughter Julia were left alone to furnish the house with family furnishings and souvenirs from their trips to Europe and the Near East.

Until 1965 the house was lived in by Bryant's descendants, and it has since been refurbished to appear as it did during Bryant's last summer there. In the elegant Victorian formal parlor, which faces the front of the house, are plush chairs, oval marbletop tables, a fireplace with blue Delft tiles, and an unusual mantel made from the original southside front door. At the end of the house is the library or study, a replica of Bryant's father's office, where Bryant and his family spent much of their time. Dr. Bryant's medical and personal libraries, as well as the poet's own collection, are in the bookcases lining the wall. There is a daguerreotype here of Dr. Bryant and his five sons. On the desk is the poet's large straw hat and an opened book, placed just as if he had stepped out for a moment. Nearby is the traveling lap desk, comparable to today's briefcase, and near the window the resting couch or "fainting couch" he often used. Bryant's desk was always three feet high with clutter and odds and ends. One family story relates that when an associate cleared his New York desk during one of his vacations it took Bryant all morning long when he returned to get the clutter to the height where it was comfortable for him to work.

The small back sitting room is set up with a chess set. Also on display are a collection of rocks which he gathered in the area, more of his books, and a case of military ornaments: a sword, epaulettes, and hat of General Abraham Goodwin, a relative who was an officer in the Revolution. In the dining room, which also faces the woods in the back of the house, is an old highboy which had been in the family since Bryant was a boy. When he bought the house back, he searched for the piece and finally found it. The mantelpiece here is fashioned from carved doors that once concealed a 1635 French "hide-a-bed." Nearby, the three-hundred-year-old Bryant family clock still ticks. The old back kitchen and pantry have been arranged as they were when Bryant was growing up, with some of the original artifacts, including the potbelly stove. The little green building next door, which was either a workhouse or potting shed, and the barn have been restored.

The second floor (originally the first floor) has four bedrooms with wide floors and closely-paned windows, and two baths, one containing a nineteenth-century tin tub and other equipment of that era. On the third floor are five small bedrooms, one of which is called the "Thanatopsis Room," since it is where the poem was supposedly written. Architecturally, the second and third floors are much the same as when Bryant arrived here as a little boy in 1799.

From all sides of the house there is a full view of the Berkshire Hills and the scenes that inspired the poems telling of his communing with nature—"To a Waterfowl," "The Fringed Gentian," and others. There is a picnic grove nearby.

Duxbury

The **Old Burying Ground** (at Hall's Corner and Chestnut St.) was a favorite haunt of Henry Wadsworth Longfellow. He often came here to stroll among the graves of Myles Standish, John Alden, and other members of the Plymouth Colony who were thought to be buried here. Longfellow, a direct descendant of John Alden, had long been attracted to Duxbury and was well versed in the history surrounding the little town.

After *The Song of Hiawatha* had become popular, Longfellow was urged to write about the Pilgrims. *The Courtship of Miles Standish,* a Puritan pastoral, was the outcome of that effort. He told his close friend Charles Sumner that the long poem of his imagined dialogue had been "founded on the well-known adventure of his maternal ancestor John Alden with Priscilla as the heroine in Duxbury.'' The slow pace of the story and the lack of passion in John Alden's lovemaking made it popular with Victorian audiences.

Alden House (Alden St. Open 9:30-5 daily, late June-Labor Day. Rest of yr. by appt. Adm. charged) was built by Jonathan Alden, third son of John and Priscilla Alden, in 1653. Longfellow often visited the home of his ancestors when he came to Duxbury.

Hampden

Laughing Brook Education Center and Wildlife Sanctuary (789 Main St. Open Tues.-Sat. 10-5, Sun. 1-5. Closed Thanks., Dec. 25, Jan. 1. Adm. charged) was home to Thornton Burgess for much of his life. From 1928 until his death at 91 in 1965, he lived and worked for part of the year at this secluded one-hundred-acre property and became one of America's most published authors. In his more than fifty years of writing stories about Laughing Brook, the Green Forest, Peter Rabbit, Reddy Frog, Grandfather Fox, and others, Burgess brought the animal world and the outdoors to a large audience of children. In all, he wrote more than seventy books and fifteen thousand stories for newspaper syndication. The Massachusetts Audubon Society has developed the property into an educational nature center where children can come to see the animals of Burgess's stories in their natural habitat. Along the many nature trails in the woods are quail, rabbits, flying squirrels, and foxes.

His doll-like Cape Cod house, filled as he left it with early Americana, is now used for tours which demonstrate various aspects of Colonial living. All the rooms have original walls, floors, and ceiling beams. Burgess bought the house because it reminded him of his boyhood home in Sandwich, Massachusetts, and used it as a summer place until 1955 when his wife died and he moved there permanently from Springfield.

The fireplace of the largest room, the old Colonial kitchen, has many candle molds, cooking implements, and foot warmers. Along the walls are shelves of Wedgwood dishes and early brown glass from Sandwich. The dining room is set up formally as it was when Burgess lived there. Though he kept the atmosphere of the house cozy and informal, he dressed for dinner each evening in coat and tie. The front parlor has many items his children brought back from their travels. In the bedroom, originally the borning room, his slippers still hang on the wall.

The barn has displays of his books, as well as original paintings by his illustrator, Harrison Cady, and an array of mounted animals, snake skins, and skeletons he collected. The pine-paneled back room of the barn, which he used as a study after arthritis kept him from climbing the hill to his studio, is now the Western Massachusetts Audubon Society office. Here are a number of his scrapbooks, copies of all of his books, all of his lectures and slides, and carbon copies of all the fifteen thousand stories. The smaller adjoining building has a number of items in glass cases.

Midway between the nature center and Burgess's studio is a gift shop, in Burgess's time the guesthouse where Cady and others stayed when they visited. His hilltop studio has been reconstructed as a classroom for the center's educational programs.

Harvard

Fruitlands Museums (Prospect Hill Rd., 2 mi. W off State Route 110. Open June-Sept., Tues.-Sun., Mon. if holiday, 1-5 P.M. Closed Oct.-May. Adm. charged; includes Fruitlands, Old Shaker House,

Picture Gallery, American Indian Museum) is a group of historic buildings which have been moved to this rural setting and restored. Fruitlands, the early eighteenth-century farmhouse where Bronson Alcott attempted to form a Utopian community in 1843, is now a museum of the Transcendentalist movement and contains books and memorabilia of its leaders—the Alcotts, Emerson, Thoreau, Margaret Fuller, Charles Lane, and others.

Bronson Alcott acted as the overseer of the group, and evidently was somewhat of a despot. Each morning he would gather the members together in the conference room and dole out the chores for the day. He himself couldn't stand hard physical labor and found an excuse to take off with Lane at one point, leaving the women and children to harvest the crops. It was impossible for them to get them all in and they almost starved. Mr. and Mrs. Alcott fought and her relatives pressured her to leave him. Soon thereafter, in its seventh month, the scheme failed and the group disbanded. Charles Lane took refuge with the Shakers and the Alcotts returned to Concord.

In the downstairs hallway are some originals of the over one thousand volumes of metaphysical works Alcott brought from England in the fall of 1842. Few pieces in the house were here during the short duration of Fruitlands, but since the Alcotts had drawn a detailed plan of the house, the curators knew how it had been furnished. In Bronson Alcott's study there is a desk similar to one he used here, and a bookcase which belonged at one time to Hawthorne.

The center of activity had been the conference or dining room, where the daily planning was done. Here on the wall is a copy of a letter Emerson wrote explaining how a commune would not be good for him. Though not part of the group, he urged Alcott to go to England to look at experimental schools and communal living arrangements. In the letter Emerson said that members of such groups must make sacrifices but that these sacrifices cannot be made without detriment to one's individuality. He suggested that the Alcott family come to his house for a year of labor and planning to straighten things out rather than plunge into an experiment with others. Mrs. Alcott, who felt strongly that the family should be an independent unit, was against this idea, and therefore they did not go to live with the Emersons. Her decision may have spurred them on to Fruitlands. She declined Emerson's offer again, after Fruitlands dissolved.

On the table in the conference room are several original copies of *The Dial,* the journal of the Transcendentalist movement which was published from 1840 to 1844. One of these issues, July 1843, has a letter from Fruitlands signed by Alcott and Lane, setting forth their aims and ambitions for the venture.

In the adjoining Manuscript Room are a number of comprehensive exhibits on various aspects of the Transcendentalist movement, many of them with original manuscripts and first editions, and all annotated to give historical perspective. Several are devoted to Bronson Alcott's theories of social reform and education, which were considered very advanced for their time. He was an "American Pestalozzi" who wanted to make school more interesting for students and have their curriculum more individualized. When he went to England he was lionized by fellow reformers for his writings, many excerpts of which can be seen in this room. At his controversial Temple School in Boston, attended by children of prominent families, he had his pupils plan their progress for the day in journals. Though it was closed by critics, it later became a prototype for the modern schoolroom.

In addition to copies of *The Dial,* the *Boston Quarterly Review,* and *The Western Messenger,* there are a number of other works by such writers as Margaret Fuller, Kate Sanborn, Ralph Waldo Emerson, and Samuel Taylor Coleridge. Especially interesting are sections from Louisa May Alcott's *Transcendental Wild Oats,* an account of the Fruitlands experiments, and pages from her Fruitlands diary. Also on exhibit are sections of Margaret Fuller's essay "Women in the Nineteenth Century," a manifesto of feminism declaring that women had all the rights of men to suffrage and careers, which first appeared in *The Dial.*

Other buildings include the Picture Gallery, noted for its early nineteenth-century itinerant portraits and Hudson River School paintings, the old Shaker House built in the 1790s by the Shakers of the former Harvard Shaker Village and furnished to illustrate Shaker life, and the American Indian Museum with prehistoric articles and other relics. Of special interest at the latter are the pieces Henry David Thoreau had collected along the Concord River.

Many of these he kept on the third floor of his parents' house at 255 Main Street in Concord, which he had filled with artifacts that he had found. Ironically, Thoreau did not think much about putting artifacts in museums; in his essays he said that we should let nature take care of our antiquities.

Haverhill

The **John Greenleaf Whittier Birthplace** (305 Whittier Rd. 3 mi. NE on State Route 110. Open 10-5, Tues.-Sat.; Sun from 1 P.M. Closed major hols. Adm. charged), still set off by itself among the rolling hills outside Haverhill, has been operating as a self-sufficient New England farm since the early 1700s when Whittier's ancestors settled here. On December 17, 1807, the eccentric local physician of Essex County, later immortalized as "the wise old doctor" of the poem "Snow-Bound," pulled up to the isolated farmhouse in a white-topped carriage to aid in the birth of the poet.

A step inside the front door makes the warmth and intimacy of rural New England come alive. Family life revolved around the large fireplace in the kitchen here, its stone floor worn smooth from six generations of use. This is the room of "Snow-Bound" where family and friends sat mesmerized by the fire as a fierce blizzard roared around the countryside and enveloped them in "a universe of sky and snow." "Shut in from all the world without," the family sat as their mugs of cider simmered and their apples baked. As the storm went on Mrs. Whittier sat at her spinning wheel and told rich and picturesque tales of her youth, of Indian raids, fishing, and nutting. Uncle Moses, who lived with them and "was rich in the lore of fields and brooks," had many hunting tales, and sweet old Aunt Mercy told of her girlhood memories of huskings, quilting bees, and sleigh rides. Whittier's schoolmaster, Joshua Coffin, from the nearby town of Newburyport, also had his favorite place at the fire. He talked of his days at Dartmouth and recited the poetry of Burns and Cowper.

It was at this hearth that the young Whittier, later to be revered as one of the country's leading Quaker humanitarians, absorbed the rich New England folklore that was to appear later in his poetry. Right on the "clean winged hearth" is all the original cooking, baking, and candlemaking equipment from generations of Whittiers. Nearby, in a hand-hewn hutch, are a number of original dishes and an original cider mug that the family of "Snow-Bound" used to warm on the fire. All the family's meals were cooked here, and material for the family's clothes was spun on the old spinning wheel. At the desk near the front door, whose step is made from an old millstone used to grind the family grain down at Fernside Brook, Whittier first started to write poetry. Behind it is the family linen chest, which has some original pieces made in the house by his mother.

This room and the small elevated bedroom behind it, built on a boulder which was much too hard to move, made up the original farmhouse built in 1688. Here are original quilts and clothes belonging to Whittier's mother, a coat of the poet's, and a number of children's clothes. The second bedroom and parlor were added later. Whittier was born in the back parlor, which also served as a guest room for the many Quakers who passed through. The small family library still remains there.

This was the world of young Whittier. He often arose at four to dress in the clothes his mother had spun for him and went out to join the hired hands. Whittier said that one of his greatest pleasures in youth was accompanying his Uncle Moses on many expeditions in the area. They often walked along Country Brook from its beginning up in the New Hampshire hills down to the Merrimack River. Joshua Coffin introduced him to the Scottish dialect of Robert Burns when he was fourteen, and from then on Whittier began to feel the need to capture his world in verse as Burns had. Soon he began to see his poems in the *Haverhill Gazette,* and after a few years of working his way through Haverhill Academy and teaching school he went on to work for papers in Boston, Hartford, and

Philadelphia. A strong antislavery advocate, he and his family often kept runaway slaves at the farmhouse.

A number of Whittier haunts are within walking distance of the house. Just outside the back door is the stone on which the barefoot boy ate his bowl of milk and bread. Whittier supposedly sat here and thought out the poem. Signs in the yard lead to the family burial ground where Whittier's ancestors lie in a plot surrounded by a stone wall, and to Fernside Brook, a tributary of Country Brook, a bit farther up on the right where there are the ruins of the old gristmill. During Whittier's time the garden extended right down to the brook, and he could cross it and climb up to the top of Job's Hill, from where he could see the blue outline of the Deerfield Mountains in New Hampshire, the peak of Agamenticus on the coast of Maine, and Kenoza Lake, which he celebrated in his poems. It was on the lake that Whittier enjoyed fishing, "the contemplative man's recreation," with his Uncle Moses.

The old Whittier barn, built by his father and Uncle Moses, is just across the road from the farmhouse. Much of it was destroyed in a recent fire but has now been rebuilt. In "Snow-Bound" this is the barn the boys had to walk to in drifts of four feet or more.

Whittier Road goes between the house and the barn and curves to the left near the top of the hill. On the left side is the site of the Whittier elm, under which Whittier used to play as a boy. He had a wooden platform built under the tree where he used to come to read and scribble in solitude. Across the street from this site is the house where his childhood friend, Lydia Ayer, the little girl who spelled the word in "In Schooldays" lived. About fifty yards ahead on the right side of the road is a large millstone which marks the site of the country schoolhouse in that poem. Whittier began attending classes at age seven, and although most of the instruction was very poor, at one point he was taught by the splendid teacher Joshua Coffin, one of the family friends in "Snow-Bound," whom he also celebrated in his poem "To My Old Schoolmaster." He described him as one who made learning a joy rather than a drudge.

Whittier-Land by Samuel T. Pickard (for sale at the Birthplace) maps out a number of Whittier sites which are located on the back roads between the Whittier Homestead, where the poet was born and spent his youth, and the Whittier Home in Amesbury, nine miles away, where he lived as an adult (see entry). Included, along with extensive background information, are homes and gravesites of characters in his poems and many other places which are part of the local tradition he drew on.

Marshfield

Winslow House (on State Route 139, at corner of Webster and Careswell Sts. Open 10-5 Wed.-Mon., July 1-Labor Day. Adm. charged) has on its grounds the last surviving building from Daniel Webster's extensive Marshfield estate. The frame house from which he practiced law, managed his livestock farm of over 1500 acres, kept a library, and met with visiting foreign dignitaries was moved here in 1966. All of the furnishings, except for the showcases, were owned by Webster. There is a working table in the middle, a desk at one end, and photos and various other documents on the plain green walls. On shelves are volumes of his speeches and other books with Webster associations.

A plaque in front of Winslow House states that it was the home of Governor Edward Careswell, and that the structure standing was constructed in 1699 on the site of the original home, which was built in 1636.

Nantucket

(Ferry from Wood's Hole. Maps and information available at Tourist Information Office, 25 Federal St., and Nantucket Historical Society, Old Town Building, Union St.). Nantucket has a number of literary associations. Melville based *Moby Dick* on a whaling incident off the island after reading an account of it by a first mate, Owen Chase, who served under Captain George Pollard. The **Peter Foulger Museum** (Broad St. next to Whaling Museum. Open late May-mid-Oct., daily 10-5; rest of yr. 2-5, Sat. Adm. charged) has a copy of Chase's version. Both Melville and Thoreau stayed at the **Jared Coffin House** (29 Broad St.) when they visited the island. Thoreau spent time here studying flora and fauna and writing about them. Both he and Melville lectured at the Athenaeum. The site of Robert Lowell's poem "The Quaker Graveyard in Nantucket" can be visited.

New Bedford

New Bedford Whaling Museum (18 Johnny Cake Hill. Exit 22 on I-195. Turn S on Union St. to Johnny Cake Hill. Open 9-5, Mon.-Sat., 1-5 Sun., June-Sept. Rest of yr. closed Mon.) is one of several buildings in the heart of the restored **Johnny Cake Hill** section that reflect the spirit of nineteenth-century New Bedford as Herman Melville knew it.

Aside from the excellent exhibits depicting life in eighteenth-and-nineteenth-century New England, the Whaling Museum has a number of paintings and etchings which illustrate whaling. Those entranced by the nautical technicalities of *Moby Dick* will enjoy the sixty-foot model of the bark *Lagoda,* typical of the whaling ships that set out from New Bedford from about 1850 to as late as 1924, and the comprehensive exhibits on whaling. Virtually every implement needed for whaling is on display here: cutting splices, harpoons, and many devices used to kill the sperm whale. In addition to its own excellent scrimshaw exhibit, the museum has on loan the late John F. Kennedy's personal collection.

Seamen's Bethel, which Melville often visited when he was in New Bedford, is across the street. In the seventh chapter of *Moby Dick* he described this chapel where the moody fishermen stopped before sailing out to the Indian Ocean. Inside the door is a photo of Melville and a plaque dedicated to him. It says that he dared to travel to the southernmost seas where he "discerned the primordial beauty and terror of this world and the danger-ridden labors of whaling and put it all into the immortal saga of *Moby Dick.''* A plaque on the outside has a quotation from Melville describing the chapel and saying that there were few sailors who failed to make this stop.

The belowground level of the Seamen's Bethel is a low-ceilinged room with simple wooden benches facing a plain altar. Here sailors came in off the street at any time of day in whatever clothes they had on. Upstairs in the regular chapel, which resembles a typical New England Congregational church, are the large memorial plaques Melville mentioned. Each one tells how the particular sailor met his fate, whether it was by "fastening whales" or by being "nipped by sharks while bathing.''

This is the Whalemen's Chapel in *Moby Dick.* It was founded in the 1830s by a wealthy city father who felt that he should give thought to the character-building of the nearly five thousand seamen who came in and out of port. The old foot-powered organ Melville mentioned is still here, and though the pulpit does not have a rope ladder leading to it like the one in the novel, it is the actual spot from which Father Mapple, based on the real minister, Enoch Mudge, preached. Mudge, a rather colorful preacher of the 1840s, at one point is said to have pushed an organ down to the docks in a wheelbarrow so that the departing sailors could have a service just as the boat was pulling out. Mapple is also thought to be partly patterned after the Transcendentalist speaker E. T. Taylor, since a picture resembling Melville's description in *Moby Dick* of a ship beating against the wind was hung behind the altar at his Boston church.

Northampton

First Church (near corner of Maine and Old South Sts.) is one of several places associated with firebrand preacher Jonathan Edwards. A memorial plaque is on the steps there. In front of the bottom step a large semicircular stone marks the entrance to the original meeting house where Edwards preached.

In his *Narrative* Jonathan Edwards described Northampton in the mid-1730s as a God-intoxicated community with every activity and conversation given over to religion. Edwards had arrived here in 1726 to assist his grandfather, Solomon Stoddard, then minister of the Congregational Church of Northampton. Soon after, he began giving his persuasive sermons on the uncertainty of life and the sinfulness of his flock, proclaiming that man was nothing and God all. After becoming a bit too fervid for the established citizens of Northampton, he was finally forced south to Stockbridge, where he did some of his finest writing. His most famous work, "Sinners in the Hands of an Angry God," was delivered in 1741 in Enfield, Connecticut.

Forbes Library (20 West St. across from the Smith College campus), known for its fine manuscript collections, has two letters

Edwards wrote in 1746, and several of his sermons. One, marked Sermon Two, April 3, 1757, begins, "Slothful servants are unprofitable servants." Among the hundreds of letters from old New England families are several written by Ralph Waldo Emerson.

Plymouth

Pilgrim Hall (Court and Chilton Sts. Open 9 A.M.-4:30 P.M. daily. Closed Dec. 25, Jan. 1. Adm. charged), a Greek revival-style building, houses a museum dedicated to the memory of the Pilgrims. Among its holdings are the famous painting "The Landing of the Pilgrims" by Henry Sargent, Governor William Bradford's Bible, which was printed in Geneva in 1592, correspondence between early Dutch and English settlers in the New World and their relatives back in Europe, and first editions of works by Winslow and Bradford. Also on display are letters of Thoreau, Emerson, Bronson Alcott, Longfellow, Whittier, among others.

Plimouth Plantation (2 mi. S of Plymouth, off State Route 3A. Open daily Apr. 1 to Nov. 30, 9-5. Adm. charged), built on the site Longfellow often visited, has re-created the early fortified village as it seems to have appeared in 1627 according to old records, eyewitness descriptions, archaeological research, and such early works as William Bradford's *Of Plimouth Plantation.* Guides in period costume lecture informally as they perform the everyday tasks necessary to maintain the farming community.

William Bradford, the farmer from Yorkshire who sailed over on the Mayflower and became the colony's first governor, wrote a journal of his adventures which remained unpublished until two hundred years after his death. *Of Plimouth Plantation,* now considered one of the major prose works of seventeenth-century American literature, details the daily life of a simple people who used all their resources in the face of adversity. Bradford describes the arrival on Cape Cod, the First Thanksgiving after successes and failures at farming, and wars with the Indians.

Rockport

Ralph Waldo Emerson Inn (1 ½ mi. N, off State Route 127): On July 23, 1855, Ralph Waldo Emerson wrote in his journal that he had just returned from the inn where he had made acquaintance with the sea. He went on to ask if it were not "a noble, friendly power who had persuaded [him] so late to make that inn and the sea his proper summer home." Until a proprietor decided to name the inn after its famous guest, it was known as the Hotel Edward.

During the 1850s only the oldest portion of the Ralph Waldo Emerson Inn existed, and the swimming pool area was covered over by rough shrubbery. At that time swimming was not yet in vogue, and climbing on the rocks was a favorite pastime. The inn was typical of coastal places where many New England writers vacationed. Now that the inn has been renamed it is visited by some for its literary association. According to records Emerson stayed in Room 109 at the top of the stairs.

Salem

The House of the Seven Gables (54 Turner St., off Derby St., together with other historic houses which have been moved here. On grounds are **Hathaway House, Hawthorne's birthplace,** and **Retire Beckett House.** Guided tours daily July-Labor Day, 9:30 A.M.-7:30 P.M.; rest of yr. 10 A.M.-4:30 P.M. Closed Thanks., Dec. 25, Jan. 1) has a mystique that few literary houses can claim. Not only is it located in a town which was the seat of witchcraft activity in the 1700s but it is also considered the subject of Nathaniel Hawthorne's enduring novel. Built in 1668 by sea captain John Turner, the House of the Seven Gables stood at another location on Turner Street until 1910, when it was restored and moved a few blocks away to its present site east of Derby's Wharf. Several generations of the Turner family lived there before it was taken over by the Ingersoll family for another few generations. By the time Hawthorne began visiting his cousin Susan Ingersoll in the 1840s the house had quite a history. He was supposedly one of the few people allowed to enter. At one point, when he was just about finishing his novel, he made a visit and was shown the attic beams and mortises which show that the structure is truly made of seven gables. Thus he had a name for his book.

Scenes from the novel come alive once you cross the threshold. The focal point is the oaken elbow dining room chair where the iron-hearted Puritan Colonel Pyncheon was suddenly grasped by death as he sat, pen in hand, with letters, parchments, and blank sheets of paper before him on the table. That momentous event occurred moments before his housewarming feast was to begin. Pyncheon had built his mansion on the site of a hut owned by simple Puritan Matthew Maule, after he had arranged for Maule to be accused, convicted, and hanged for witchcraft. He then razed

Maule's hut and built his own magnificent mansion. As Maule died he put a curse on Pyncheon which was to visit Pyncheon and his descendants.

Visitors still walk through the shop door with its overhanging tinkle bell where the wizened old spinster Hepzibah sold her penny wares in an attempt to retrieve the family fortune. In the novel, Hepzibah and her cousin Phoebe were running a scent shop in front of the house, which was one of many weatherbeaten structures on either side of Turner Street. Also here was Hepzibah's brother Clifford, who had just returned home, feeble and infirm after being unjustly imprisoned for thirty years for the alleged murder of his rich Uncle Pyncheon, a descendant of the original Colonel Pyncheon. Clifford's cousin, Judge Pyncheon, who was responsible for having Clifford imprisoned, then accused him of taking large sums of money from his rich uncle's estate and threatened to put him in an asylum unless he gave clues to the money's whereabouts. At that point Judge Pyncheon died in his chair with the curse of Maule upon him, just as his ancestor Colonel Pyncheon had. It was through the small window on the opposite side of the room that the butcher boy noticed him slumped over. Hepzibah and Clifford were then free. Nearby is the old Colonial kitchen where the servants of the house prepared the great feasts for Colonel Pyncheon.

In the large formal parlor, the Pyncheons' grand reception room, the desk on which Hawthorne wrote when he came still stands. At one point he is said to have been talking to his cousin about an apparent writer's block. She then looked at one of the large straight-backed chairs in this room and suggested he use it as a subject, since it was called the Grandfather Chair. A short time later he came out with a group of stories, *Tales from a Grandfather's Chair.* Above the spinet piano in this room is a portrait of Hawthorne at age 36. In a cupboard beside the fireplace is a picture of a character in *The House of the Seven Gables,* the artist Holgrave, who lodged here with Hepzibah in the novel. Behind a panel on the other side is the secret doorway leading up the famous narrow stairway to a hidden panel behind the fireplace in Clifford's room. On the day of the judge's death Hepzibah came up through this passage in search of her brother. She paused by the window and looked down into the garden where he often sat on a circular summer seat. Phoebe's room of the novel is in a corner of the large east chamber. The upstairs rooms ramble on and on and are all decorated in the style of the period of the novel.

Just how much the house of the novel is a composite of this and other places Hawthorne visited is not known. In the preface his comment that Pyncheon owned most of Waldo County, Maine, leads one to believe that he was referring to the lavish estate of General Knox (see Thomaston, Maine), whom Hawthorne visited. He also spoke of "building a house of material long in use" and of "constructing castles in the air." Hawthorne mentions the Family Annals at the beginning of the novel. He had read many such family histories from the witchcraft era of the late 1600s while working at the Custom House. At the time he was gathering materials for *The House of the Seven Gables,* the house stood on Turner Street with a number of other old weather-beaten structures. The combination of his romantic bent and his knowledge of the Puritan era may well have enabled him to blend the old Salem legends into one single work of art. Materials from the novel no doubt came from many interwoven sources. It is also interesting to note that one of Hawthorne's ancestors was a witch judge and that the husband of a woman whom he had persecuted severely pronounced a curse on the Hawthorne family. That ancestor, John Hathorne (original spelling of family name), also persecuted a Philip English, and the two became enemies. However, Hathorne's son married one of the English daughters, thereby ending the long-standing quarrel. That union could have planted a seed in Hawthorne's mind for the marriage of Phoebe and Holgrave, which ended the Pyncheon-Maule feud of several generations. Hawthorne also must have read about the celebrated murder case of a wealthy Mr. White, who had been killed by a man White's nephew had hired. Daniel Webster was called in as prosecutor. The relationship between that incident and the novel is quite obvious.

Salem in Hawthorne's day was just beginning to decline as a major port. However, it was still filled with those who made their living by the sea, with wizened old maids like Hepzibah who stayed secluded in their houses, and with legends galore of those in past generations who had been executed for witchcraft. There were many family stories of various houses which had been cursed, and an impressive and imaginative young mind such as Hawthorne's made a lot of that.

When Hawthorne was four, his uncle, William Manning, built a house for the boy and his widowed mother in the wilderness of Raymond, Maine (see entry). The Hawthornes then left Salem and lived in Maine until they felt that young Nathaniel needed a more cosmopolitan area to prepare for college. When he returned to Salem at age fifteen he worked in his uncle's coach offices several hours each morning, spent the early afternoon being tutored in Greek and Latin, and in his leisure time roamed around the countryside, often walking up to Gallows Hill where he found solitude to do his own reading. Here he discovered the Arthurian tales, the *Arabian Nights,* Godwin's novels, and Sir Walter Scott, and also continued to work on the poetry he had begun in Maine. When Hawthorne was a young boy his uncle had given him a notebook and told him to write down systematic observations of things in preparation for some profession ahead. That got the young Hawthorne going on the many notebooks he was to keep throughout his life. After graduating from Bowdoin College in the same class with Franklin Pierce and Henry Wadsworth Longfellow, he returned to Salem and led a rather austere life for twelve years, working when he needed money as a measurer in the Custom House and devoting himself to writing. During this time he really developed his gift for prose and established himself as an author with *Twice-Told Tales.* He then lived in a worn-down house, now demolished, on Herbert Street, spending most of his time writing by day and roaming the streets at night.

In 1842 Hawthorne married Sophia Peabody, also of Salem, and moved to Concord (see entry), where they lived for a few years in the Old Manse, built in 1769 by the grandfather of Ralph Waldo Emerson. His collection of short stories, *Mosses from an Old Manse,* chronicles their life there. When funds ran out, he returned to Salem and worked again at the Custom House for a few years and lived at a house which still stands at 14 Mall Street.

Hawthorne's birthplace, built by his grandfather from a seventeenth-century kitchen, was recently moved here from 27 Union Street. Though none of the furniture is from the family, it is decorated to reflect the kind of background he was born into. There are a parlor, child's room, spinning room, the borning room, and master bedroom with canopy bed. The old kitchen from which the house was built has the traditional work table, hutch, dry sink, and cradle. The **Retire Beckett** House, for six generations a home of ship designers and builders, now serves as a gift shop. Adjoining it is the **Hathaway House,** which for two hundred years had been a famous old New England bakery.

Custom House (Derby St., opposite Derby Wharf. Open daily July-Labor Day, 8:30 A.M.-7 P.M.; rest of yr. to 5 P.M. Closed Thanks., Dec. 25, Jan. 1. Free), a majestic brick building topped with a gilded eagle, was the hub of activity when Hawthorne worked here from 1846 to 1849. At that time the area was built up with warehouses, and many vessels docked at the wharf. In the introduction to his most widely read novel, *The Scarlet Letter,* Hawthorne describes the Custom House and its surroundings. Just inside is the room which Hawthorne used as his office when he worked as a surveyor of the port. Here are his standing desk, three-legged stool, inkwell, and pens. From the window he could see the port and Derby Street, then lined with the shops of Salem's chandlers and shipbuilders. A recording describes the room and view during his stay. Here he made notes and outlines for *The Scarlet Letter.* When the job became too oppressive for him he left Salem for good and retired for about eighteen months to the country (see Lenox, Massachusetts), where he wrote the novel and refreshed himself before settling at The Wayside (see Concord, Massachusetts).

Grimshawe House (53 Charter St. Privately owned and not open to the public), which Hawthorne described in *Dr. Grimshawe's Secret,* still stands. This was the former house of his wife Sophia Peabody, known as one of "the Peabody sisters of Salem."

Longfellow's *New England Tragedies* dealt with one of the Salem witches. Also, Arthur Miller's *The Crucible* was set during the witchcraft era, and Maxwell Anderson wrote of the town in *Wingless Victory.*

South Sudbury

The **Wayside Inn** (off US 20. Museum rooms open 9-6 daily. Adm. charge to nonguests) takes its name from the long poem *Tales of a Wayside Inn,* which Henry Wadsworth Longfellow composed while vacationing here. Early in this century Henry Ford, realizing that the inn had become a popular literary shrine, bought thousands of surrounding acres and restored the inn as Longfellow knew it. He even went so far as to have paved roads detoured several hundred feet away so as not to destroy the setting. All cars are now kept in a parking lot several hundred feet away from the entrance.

Longfellow, no doubt, was part of the group which sat around the fireplace here listening to innkeeper Lyman How's (spelled **Howe** by future generations) tales of his grandfather's adventures during the Revolution. After Lyman How died in 1861 a group of college professors who often spent summer vacations here encouraged Longfellow to write down the tales. The result of that endeavor was *Tales of a Wayside Inn,* which came out in 1863. The tales, as Longfellow rendered them, included those of a theologian, a student, a poet, a musician, a Spanish Jew, and a Sicilian. Innkeeper How is featured as the landlord and speaks the most well-known lines of the poem, "Listen, my children, and you will hear. . .''

Near the turn of the century, as Longfellow's poems made the place famous, the inn's name was changed from Red Horse Tavern to the Wayside Inn. About this time formal gardens were added and antiques were bought. One coaching company offered package day trips from Boston for $6.50. This included the round trip, a tour of Longfellow's parlor and bedroom, and a meal and drink at the inn. Guests also came on bicycles, and in sleighs and carriages. At that time kerosene lanterns hung from the ceilings to provide light for the musicians. In addition to the Longfellow Parlor are the old kitchen and barroom, several old early American bedrooms, including one in which Lafayette supposedly slept, and a number of other guest rooms.

It was in the spacious Longfellow Parlor that the poet pictured his friends sitting around the fire telling their tales, "the firelight shedding all over/the splendor of its ruddy glow." The large room is decorated with period furniture and a few pieces from the Long-fellow family. There is a desk from Longfellow's grandfather's home in Hiram, Maine, a family Bible, and a Bible box in front of one of the windows. In frames above a chest are original panes of window glass etched and signed by Major Molineux, a poem, and a picture of a princess mentioned in one of Longfellow's poems. On the back wall is the simple fireplace which made this room famous and in the front corner an early nineteenth-century pianoforte, one of the first in the area. In the middle of the room are a round table and four chairs where the guests used to sit, bathed in the light of the fire.

Upstairs is the Longfellow chamber, one of the rooms of a 1716 addition, decorated as it was when the poet stayed here. Next to the fireplace here is a rocking chair with a candlestick beside it. Nearby is a traveling desk; it is like the one Longfellow would have used while working late at night, after socializing downstairs earlier in the evening.

Henry Ford brought other buildings to the Wayside and restored them. On the grounds is the "Mary Had a Little Lamb" School-house, originally from the nearby town of Sterling. According to local legend Mary Sawyer took a sick lamb to school and hid it beneath her desk. The animal came out of hiding when Mary was called to recite in front of the class. Many New England towns claim to own the original schoolhouse of the poem. (See Newport, New Hampshire.) Also on the grounds are the Mary-Martha Chapel, a classic white New England church, and a working eighteenth-century gristmill which grinds flour and meal for the kitchens at the inn.

Springfield

The **Springfield Armory National Historic Site** (Federal St., on grounds of Springfield Technical Community College. Open Mon.-Sat. 10A.M.-5P.M.; Sun. and hols. from 1P.M.; closed Thanks., Dec. 25, Jan. 1) was known as the Springfield Arsenal when Henry Wadsworth Longfellow used to come here and, as he said, "bathe in the aura of history." At that time the original building, a few doors down from the present museum, was filled from floor to ceiling with guns stacked side by side. In his poem "The Arsenal at Springfield" he wrote: "This is the arsenal. From floor to ceiling,/ Like a huge organ, rise the burnished arms." These percussion-lock guns were the main type of firearm used during the Civil War by both North and South. In Longfellow's day, of course, this was where the guns were stored for actual use. The Armory has one of the original "organs" prominently displayed in the center of the museum room. Excerpts from poems by poets who drew their inspiration from exhibits here are on placards near the "organ" and on the surrounding walls.

NEW HAMPSHIRE

Crawford Notch

Hawthorne drew upon the well-known Willey tragedy at Crawford Notch for one of his most popular short stories, "The Ambitious Guest." While visiting this valley in the White Mountains he was awestruck by the beauty of the high crags above the Saco River. He also saw the huge ledge of rock which had rushed past the Willey house, leaving it untouched while the surrounding fields were covered by huge boulders and fallen trees.

That storm on August 28, 1826, was the most violent and destructive ever known in the White Mountains. The river rose twenty-four feet, farms were set afloat, and gorges were cut into mountainsides. Several days later, when friends and relatives penetrated the debris-strewn valley to discover the fate of the Willey family, they found the house untouched. From all appearances the family had left hurriedly to run from the avalanche and escape to a nearby cave. Soon after, the bodies of the hired men and most of the family were found crushed in the wreckage. Hawthorne and other writers have speculated on the causes of their ironic fate.

Each summer visitors make their way to the Willey memorial, a small stone on the site of the house. The park manager's office has pictures of the original house, a painting done after the landslide, a photograph of the Willey grave at Intervale, and a few pieces of memorabilia from the avalanche.

Derry

The **Robert Frost Farm** (on State Route 28, ¼ mi. S of junction of Route 28 and Bypass 28. Open 9-5, Wed.-Sun., June 21-Labor Day; weekends, Memorial Day-June 21 and Labor Day-Columbus Day) consists of a simple New England house and barn which stand off to the side of a winding country road near Derry. Biographers now realize how much Frost's years here from 1901 to 1909 laid the foundation for the great body of poetry he wrote. He came to the farm at age 28 and got his start as a poet as he tilled the land.

Both buildings are being restored with the aid of the recollections of Frost's daughter Leslie, the first of the Frost children to be born here. The interior of the house has been simply decorated with furniture similar to the Frosts'. In the middle of the front parlor, for example, is the woodburning stove around which the family gathered on winter evenings to read to each other. One of the few original possessions is *The Scottish Chiefs,* the first book Frost owned. Considerable work has been done to restore the farm kitchen, with its soapstone sink and walk-in pantry, to its original condition.

Frost was not the typical New England farmer who toiled from dawn to dusk. All the while he was going through the mechanics of farming, his mind was really on poetry. Whenever the details of everyday life became too tedious, he would turn to his own world of speculation "to smell the earth" or "look into the center of the ant,'' as he described his productive daydreaming. His usual routine was to milk the cows around midnight so that he would have the quiet of the early morning to think and write. After the chores were done, he would sit with his kerosene lamp reading Shakespeare or Vergil, or writing in his notebooks. If the mood struck him, he would take a walk out to see the moon or smell the new-mown hay before putting out his flame and going to sleep. This was a working schedule he kept for most of his life.

Many poems of his first volume, *A Boy's Will,* describe life in the area and the effect of changing seasons on the land. Others reflect domestic life within the farmhouse and reveal his wife Eleanor's role as childbearer and housekeeper. During the first six years there, six Frost children were born and two died as infants. It was a life of self-imposed isolation. During their entire stay, the family never ate a meal at a neighbor's or ''shared chores,'' a common practice among farmers in the area.

The Frosts often took rides around the remote countryside with its abandoned farms. The house was just down from the well-traveled coach road which ran from Concord, New Hampshire, to Boston, some forty miles south. To the east was the south wall which separated Frost's property from his French-Canadian neighbor's. Many times he would notice sites which were later to become images in his poetry. There was, for example, the black tarn near an abandoned farmhouse, which he imagined might be a place where suicides were committed, the west-running brook where the first Scotch-Irish settlers came and built their homes, and a picturesque cottage nearby with historic legends attached to it.

It was during 1905 and 1906 that Frost really began to develop his poetry. Two of the most moving poems in American literature were written at this time—''Home Burial,'' a composite of the Frosts' experiences and those of others who had lost children, and ''The Death of the Hired Man.'' These poems were written as he began to realize the pressures of supporting four children on his minuscule inheritance and the proceeds from the farm. In the spring of 1905 his house was almost repossessed, and soon after that incident he completed those poems which had long been germinating in his mind.

The next year Frost was offered a teaching position at nearby

Pinkerton Academy, a two-mile walk from the farm. Through the urgings of several friends in Derry, one a minister, another a businessman and community leader, he had read his poem "Tuft of Flowers" at a meeting of the Derry Village Men's Club. The group was so moved by the reading that the teachers who were there convinced him he should come to the old Romanesque building and teach English.

From that time on he did very little farming, spending his time on teaching and poetry. After he was at the academy for a year, the family moved to an old house in town so that Frost could walk to school. He became very involved with sports, drama, and field trips and was supposedly well-liked by the students, though many of the townspeople found his teaching methods too progressive. He was very informal, friendly, and unconventional in the teaching of his classes, while the school was very formal and old-fashioned. At the end of his second year there the principal claimed that he was one of the best teachers in the state because of his original classroom methods, and had the commissioner of education send him up to the State Normal School at Plymouth to teach education and psychology to prospective teachers.

All this time both his poetry and teaching were intertwined; however, the urge to write gradually became the stronger of the two. Though his job was secure at Plymouth and his family much better off than they had ever been, he decided he really needed to devote all his time to his writing and gave up the job after one year. He then sold the farm at Derry and moved to England where he farmed in Staffordshire and became friends with the English poet Edward Thomas. Two and a half years later he returned to America, this time recognized as one of America's leading modern poets.

Many of Frost's favorite spots are within walking distance of the house. The remnants of the stone wall which went around his entire property can be seen by walking south of the house and barn and down to the bed of Hyla Brook on the same side of the road. The stone wall was just beyond the brook before the incline called Klein's or Guay's Hill. At that time the area was not so wooded and overgrown. The wall continued around the bed of the brook and then went up toward the house and barn again. In back of the barn were hen houses, then an orchard and the mowing field before the gate and stone wall. Beyond that was the old South Road which the Frost family used to take to Londonderry.

Across the street from the house and to the right of the road was
Nat Head's Woods. To the left of the road were several pastures
surrounded by stone walls. Just outside the southern perimeter
of the walls was Merriam's Cellar Hole. It was the southeastern
part of the stone wall near the present main road, on the same side
as the house, which provided the images for his poem "Mending
Wall." The house and farm of Napoleon Guay, who had bought
the property from Joseph Klein, was just a little beyond the brook
and over the hill. In the poem Mr. Guay is referred to as the neighbor
he knows beyond the hill, and in "The Axe-Helve" he is Baptiste
who captures Frost's ax as it is "on the rise."

Frost spent a lot of time teaching his children about a number
of the wildflowers which appear as images in his first volumes of
poetry. He also taught them how to bend birch trees into swings,
a skill he himself learned when he was growing up in Salem, New
Hampshire, just south of Derry.

Franconia

Frost Place (Ridge Road. House open Tues.-Sat. 10-12, 1-4.
Adm. charged. Friday evening programs in barn, 8 P.M., July and
August), where the Frost family spent summers and vacations from
1915 to 1920, is now restored as an arts center and has been decorated
with furniture, photographs, and literary mementos to evoke Frost's
early life here. Each summer a poet-in-residence, chosen by *The
Atlantic Monthly,* an early publisher of Frost's poems, lives in the
house, which still has the original narrow doors and windowpanes.
In the parlor is a replica of a Frost desk and a leather-covered Morris
chair which was a favorite of his when he came here. Upstairs in
Frost's bedroom his own writing desk is set under the window. His
favorite working spot, however, was the downstairs porch, with its

full view of the mountains. In September 1920, after Frost left Amherst and had lived here for six months, he suddenly moved to another house in South Shaftsbury, Vermont. According to biographer Elizabeth Shepley Sergeant (*Robert Frost: Trial by Existence,* Holt, Rinehart, 1960), Frost's neighbors resented the sophisticated authors and professors who visited the house. Frost, feeling torn between living in the country and his academic friends, decided that he ought to leave.

The barn, where the Frosts kept two cows, a small Morgan horse, and a few chickens, now has a full summer program of concerts, lectures, and theatrical readings. Outside, a "poetry trail" leads through the orchards, white birches, evergreens, and wildflowers which inspired him during these very productive years. While at Franconia he wrote his third book of poems, *Mountain Interval,* and most of his fourth, the Pulitzer Prize-winning collection *New Hampshire.* Three of his most familiar poems—"The Road Not Taken," "Birches," and "Stopping by Woods on a Snowy Evening"— appeared in those collections.

Franklin

The **Daniel Webster Birthplace** (4 mi. SW of Franklin on State Route 127, then ½ mi. W at signs. Open May 30-mid-Oct., daily 9-6. Adm. charged) is a replica of the two-room cabin where Webster, the ninth of the ten children of Ebenezer Webster and his wife, was born in 1782. Ebenezer was a robust soldier and frontiersman who had been a commander in the French and Indian and Revolutionary wars. After coming here to settle in the western Vermont hills, he kept a tavern in nearby Salisbury, ran saw and grist mills on nearby Punch Creek, and in addition held a number of public offices in town.

The birthplace reflects the early struggles of the family rather than the world of the older Daniel Webster.

Most of young Webster's education was from newspapers, the Bible, and his parents' worldly knowledge. At thirteen he had a job as an errand boy in a local law office. He picked up Latin grammar so well that his employer insisted he go off to Exeter, where he attended for several semesters before family funds ran low and he was forced to drop out. Then, after enrolling at a preparatory school closer to home, he taught school in the area until a local minister offered to prepare him for Dartmouth where he became known as an outstanding public speaker.

He went on to practice law in Portsmouth, arguing the famous Dartmouth College case at Exeter before taking it to the Supreme Court. Though he became very successful as a lawyer and was known as one of the country's leading orators, Webster frequently returned to the area to visit old neighbors and boyhood friends.

The cabin, set inside fenced-in grounds owned and maintained by the Webster Birthplace Foundation, which purchased fifteen of the original Webster farm acres, is decorated with simple housekeeping tools and farm articles which the family would have had. There are also volumes of Webster's speeches and some other memorabilia. The exact dates that the family lived here are not known.

Hanover

Webster Cottage (North Main St. Open June-mid-Oct., Tues., Thurs., Sat., Sun. 3-5 P.M.; rest of yr. Sat. only, 2-4. Closed major hols. Free), where Daniel Webster took room and board as an undergraduate at Dartmouth College, has been restored by the local historical society and decorated with furniture of the period and a few pieces once owned by Webster. It is a typical one-story, eighteenth-century farmhouse with several garret bedrooms upstairs. A steep staircase leads up to the alcove where Webster lived and studied.

The right front room downstairs, used as a bedroom in the days when the house was a dormitory, is now furnished as a sitting room and library, with Webster memorabilia on display. Next to the fireplace is a large black leather barrel chair from his home in Franklin, New Hampshire. A commemorative stamp, one of his inkstands, a number of nineteenth-century books of the kind he no doubt had in his library, and bound volumes of his speeches, one with his autograph, are on shelves here.

The cottage was built in 1780 by the Reverend Sylvanus Ripley on a fifteen-acre lot. He lived here until he built a larger home, now Choate House, and extended his property to include one hundred acres of land which stretched down to the river. After the Ripley family left the area Choate House became a tavern and the Webster cottage was rented out to various tenants until 1836, when it was opened as a boarding house to students. Before being moved to this location in 1955, it stood on a spot next to the computer building on Main Street.

Writer Kate Sanborn also lived here while her father was a professor at Dartmouth, as did Henry Fowle Durant, the founder of Wellesley College. Some books from the Sanborn family are in the house and the Durant bedroom is furnished with family pieces on loan from Wellesley.

Newport

"The Schoolhouse" (on Concord-Claremont Rd. in hamlet of Guild. Open Sun. afternoons in summer), where the original "Mary Had a Little Lamb" incident is said to have taken place 135 years ago, is visited by thousands each year. The author of the famous poem was Sarah Josepha Hale, a pupil at the school, who later became the first American woman to make her living by writing.

Children attended the little school for almost a century after the famous incident. However, in 1891, when the building was abandoned for a new and larger one up on the hill, it was sold to a farmer who added rooms to the second floor, a woodshed, and a barn. With all the renovations done since then, the original structure would be impossible to identify were it not for the wooden ornament high on the front gable.

While many communities have claimed to own the original schoolhouse where Mary came with the lamb, the local historical society claims that this building is about thirty years older than the other ones, which had not yet been built when the poem came out. In addition, Sarah Josepha Hale's son Horatio wrote a letter to the New Hampshire *Argus Spectator* in 1889, stating that his mother was the Mary of the poem. In the introduction to her small book, *Poems for Our Children,* first published in 1830, Mrs. Hale wrote that she had written the poems to please and instruct the children who would read them. The second poem of that collection is "Mary Had a Little Lamb." When a rival legend appeared in the 1870s claiming that a student had composed the poem in honor of his teacher, a Mrs. Mary Sawyer Tyler, one of Mrs. Hale's children wrote to the magazine in which this story appeared saying that her mother was not well enough to reply, but wanted the editors to know that every poem in the book was her own composition. She also pointed out that pet lambs were very common at the time and that the incident may have happened on more than one occasion.

Sarah Josepha Buell, the daughter of a Revolutionary War officer, had married David Hale, a young, self-educated attorney and scholar who encouraged her to write and financed the publication of her first book of poems. He died suddenly soon after the birth of their fifth child. After an unsuccessful venture with a millinery shop, she began writing seriously to support her family. Five years after her husband's death, after the success of her first novel, she had become an established literary figure, and was thus invited to become the editor of the *Ladies' Magazine,* a Boston publication. Against the advice of friends and family, she moved her children to Boston to assume her editorial duties. She later moved on to Philadelphia to edit *Godey's Lady's Book,* a monthly miscellany known especially for fashion illustrations.

Peterborough

The **MacDowell Colony** (MacDowell Rd., N of town. Welcomes visitors at the main building, Colony Hall, 2-5, Mon.-Sat.) started by the widow of composer Edward MacDowell on the grounds of the secluded farm where he had come to live and compose, is now a 500-acre working retreat for professional writers, artists, and musicians, who come to work in the twenty-eight individual cabin-studios, each of which is protected from noise and interference. Every attempt is made to provide the artists with complete seclusion.

Beyond the central part of the colony (studios set in the woods) are almost four hundred acres of well-kept farmland, which spread across to Mount Monadnock.

A number of writers have received the Pulitzer Prize for works they either wrote or began here: Edward Arlington Robinson for his *Collected Poems* and *The Man Who Died Twice;* Willa Cather for *One of Ours;* Thornton Wilder for *The Bridge of San Luis Rey, Our Town* (set in Grover's Corners, which is based on Peterborough), and *The Skin of Our Teeth;* and Stephen Vincent Benét for *John Brown's Body* and *Western Star.*

Portsmouth

The **Thomas Bailey Aldrich House** (386 Court St. Open weekdays, 10-5, June-Sept. Adm. charged) has been furnished to the minutest detail as Aldrich described it in his novel *The Story of a Bad Boy,* which was immediately a popular work when it came out in 1870. This is the Nutter house where the fictional character that Aldrich named Tom Bailey lived with his Grandfather Nutter.

The typical mid-Victorian city house has large rooms, rich woodcarvings, cornices at the doors and windows, and wallpaper with large landscapes and sea views. Aside from a few family portraits and articles about Aldrich on the walls, the interior is almost as the family left it. Through the back entrance is the kitchen with a large window overlooking the back garden. The open hearth, around which members of the family often gathered, looks ready for use.

The focal point, however, is the tiny bedroom which figures so largely in the novel. This is the Bad Boy's room at the top of the stairs. Aldrich is known to have been a dreamer and an avid reader as a child and this room was his sanctuary. In one passage of the novel he describes all the books he had here. On the shelf above the bed are some of his favorites: *Robinson Crusoe, Tristram Shandy,* and *The Arabian Nights,* among others. Many times he would steal up to his room, and taking a worn volume off the shelf, slip into another world where, as he put it, there were "no lessons to get and no boys to smash my kite." Here also is his gun on the wall, his high-backed chair, his china dog, candles, and marbles. On the bed a clean vest has been laid out for him. This is the eight-foot-square room from which he lowered himself one July 4th.

Both Aunt Abigail's and Grandfather's bedrooms remain the same, hers with sewing materials scattered about and his with his Bible spread open on a table in front of his reading chair.

The third-floor attic where Aldrich played is open to view. On one side the drapes he and his friends used as a stage curtain for their theater productions still hang. Arranged around the sides under the rafters are such treasures as the family cradle, a spinning wheel, various guns, crinolines, and hoops, and a set of nineteenth-century Farmer's Almanacs. In Aldrich's day this room was always full of broken-down furniture and old clothing which the boys used as props for their plays. Aldrich used to come here alone at times to hear the rain pattering on the roof or to read his books. He lived in the house until he left for college. Later on he became a successful editor and writer in New York and Boston and at one point was editor of *The Atlantic Monthly.*

The brick museum attached to the back of the house was built by the city of Portsmouth in 1930 to house the possessions of Aldrich, the adult poet and writer, so that those would be separate from the house of the Bad Boy. On display here are manuscripts, autographs, first editions, pictures, and bric-a-brac brought from his home in Boston. This collection indicated how well known he was during his lifetime. There is a cigar case from Henry Wadsworth Longfellow, an elaborate silver bird from a rajah of India, and rosary beads from the Pope.

Nearby in **Strawbery Banke,** the newly restored early maritime community, is the small house where Daniel Webster lived when he practiced law in Portsmouth and was a representative to the United States Congress. Now the research library of Strawbery Banke, it is open by appointment.

The **Isles of Shoals** (10 mi. off the coast; frequent ferries) were a summer meeting place for many well-known writers of the nineteenth century. Among those who vacationed on these rocky islands were Thomas Bailey Aldrich, novelist Annie Fields, Nathaniel Hawthorne and his son Julian, Thomas Wentworth Higginson, the Boston minister and author who was literary mentor to Emily Dickinson (see Amherst, Massachusetts), William Dean Howells, Sarah Orne Jewett, poet John Greenleaf Whittier and his friend Lucy Larcom, and James Russell Lowell.

Summering literati often gathered in the parlor of Celia Thaxter, a year-round resident who had published a number of pieces in *The Atlantic,* and had become a recognized poet by the age of twenty-five. She also wrote the definitive book on the islands, *Among the Isles of Shoals.* Nathaniel Hawthorne called her the Miranda of the islands and said she was a charming hostess. Guests stayed either at private homes or at the Appledore Hotel, a huge white seafront structure which stood up on the rocks and was the focal point of the isles. The terrain is now sprinkled with a few white cabins and several large old hotels used as conference centers by the Unitarian Church.

Mark Twain Memorial, Hartford, Connecticut

MARK TWAIN MEMORIAL

Monte Cristo Cottage, boyhood home of Eugene O'Neill, New London, Connecticut

O'NEILL THEATRE CENTER, WATERFORD, CONN.

John Dickinson Mansion, Dover, Delaware

Montpelier, Thomaston, Maine, home of Gen. Henry Knox, said to be the model for Gen. Pyncheon of Hawthorne's *The House of the Seven Gables*

Edgar Allan Poe Monument and Grave, Baltimore, Maryland

Barbara Fritchie House, Frederick, Maryland

DIV. OF TOURIST DEVELOPMENT,
MD. DEPT. OF ECONOMIC & COMMUNITY DEVELOPMENT

Dickinson Homestead, Amherst, Massachusetts

Longfellow Home, Cambridge, Massachusetts

Ralph Waldo Emerson House, Concord, Massachusetts

MIKE ROBERTS COLOR PRODUCTIONS, BERKELEY, CAL.

Bronson Alcott's School of Philosophy at Orchard House, Concord, Massachusetts

ORCHARD HOUSE

The House of the Seven Gables, Salem, Massachusetts

HOUSE OF THE SEVEN GABLES

Pierpont Morgan Library, New York City

Zane Grey's desk, Zane Grey Museum, Lackawaxen, Pennsylvania

MARGARET KARCH ZAIMES

Edgar Allan Poe House, Philadelphia, Pennsylvania

EMILIE C. HARTING

Mohegan Bluffs, Block Island, Rhode Island, site of the wreck of the
Palatine of Whittier's poem "The Palatine Light"

The Old Stone Mill in Touro Park, Newport, Rhode Island, associated
with Longfellow's poem "A Skeleton in Armor"

NEW JERSEY

Burlington

The **James Fenimore Cooper Birthplace** (457 High St. Open Sun. 2-4. Free) is a red brick Colonial building which the family lived in before his father, William Cooper, went off to the wilderness of central New York State and founded the village of Cooperstown (see entry). The author was born in 1789 and spent his first fourteen months here. Furnished with antiques from the Burlington area, the birthplace has only one piece which actually belonged to the Coopers—a bedwarmer which survived the fire at their Cooperstown home, Otsego Hall, in 1853. However, there is a considerable amount of Cooper memorabilia in the large parlor. In display cases against the wall are first editions with hand-painted illustrations of *The Deerslayer* and *The Last of the Mohicans*. There are also pictures of the author and his family, a complete set of his works, etchings which were used as illustrations for his books, and samplers depicting scenes from his novels.

Camden

In the **Walt Whitman Home** (330 Mickle St., off 3rd St., east of Benjamin Franklin Bridge. Open 10-12 and 1-5, Tues.-Sat.; 2-5 Sun. Closed Thanks., Dec. 25, Jan. 1. Adm. charged) there are many etchings and paintings of Walt Whitman as he looked during his last years in Camden. Most cast him in a relaxed pose, his long hair and beard flowing, his muslin shirt unbuttoned. To those who did not know him as a serious poet, he was a pleasant eccentric who attracted people. Many times folks came by hoping to catch a glimpse of the good gray poet, as he was popularly known, sitting in his chair at the front window of his row house on Mickle Street.

Whitman settled in Camden after having spent many years in Washington, D.C., where he was a clerical worker for the government and served as a volunteer in army hospitals in addition to working on his war journals and poems. He came at first to visit his dying mother, who lived nearby on Stevens Street with his brother, Colonel George Whitman. After suffering a stroke, Walt found it impossible to return to Washington and stayed with George until he purchased the place on Mickle Street, where he lived until his death. He convinced Mary O. Davis, the widow of a sea captain, to bring the contents of her house and live with him as a housekeeper. Until the last years, when he had a male nurse, she not only cooked and cleaned but also helped him up and down stairs.

It seems that Whitman never had quite enough money to support himself. In Washington he had been living on a clerk's salary and modest royalties and spent any excess money, including gifts from friends, to buy supplies for the patients he nursed. He had also been sending money to his widowed mother and an invalid brother. His only real possessions when he came to Camden were the bed his father had made him, his chair, and a packing box full of books.

From time to time writers both here and in England sent him "purses" of money so that he could get by.

The Walt Whitman Home is one of three small row houses which remain standing as an oasis amid concrete highways and vacant lots, the many networks of brick row houses on tree-lined streets which made up nineteenth-century Camden having been flattened for urban renewal. Those were the streets of bustling Camden Walt used to stroll through before the last few years, when he was unable to get around on his own. The depot and ferry were close by and the railroad tracks only a mile away. There was noise and odor from a nearby guano factory, and the cobblestone streets were always grimy with soot from the nearby coalyards. A reminder of that era is the stone footrest near the curb. This was installed so that he could alight easily from his carriage after the first stroke left him partially paralyzed. Before his second stroke incapacitated him, Walt often rode the ferry between Camden and Philadelphia.

A step inside the front door is a step back into Whitman's world. It is almost as if he had never left, or perhaps as if he had stepped out for a few minutes and his housekeeper had cleared the clutter. The first room to the left from the small front hallway is the parlor which served as his study until he was confined to his bedroom for the last few years. In front of the window is the huge rocking chair he sat in to read and entertain friends. Next to the fireplace is a photograph of the neighborhood as it was when he lived here. The decor looks more like that of a rooming house than a private home, with its drab wallpaper, painted floorboards, and plain curtains. During Whitman's lifetime this room was always in complete disarray with piles of newspapers and letters and bundles of manuscripts all over. It was an editor's sanctum that smelled of printer's ink, where he altered and revised his poetry. Biographers say that he had things in constant disorder while Mrs. Davis was constantly attempting to put things in order.

The rear of the parlor is filled with photographs of Whitman and his family and several cases of personal effects, letters, and articles. Many of the family letters on display give an indication of life here with Mrs. Davis, his male nurse Warren Fitzgerald, and his recorder Horace Traubel, who came almost daily for the last three years of Whitman's life. The notes which Traubel wrote eventually became the five-volume work *With Walt Whitman in Camden.* Many visitors come especially to see the lock of gray hair in the display case at the left. There are also a number of copies of *Leaves of Grass* (including one first edition), which he first published in 1855 in Brooklyn. In Whitman's time this area served as a kitchen, dining room, and sitting room, where Mrs. Davis spent a lot of time and had a sewing corner. In a little passage between this house and the one adjoining it she kept a laundry. The rear portion of the house had a small apartment with kitchen below and sleeping room above. In good weather Whitman spent time sitting out in the backyard where there was a small shed and a pear tree for shade.

In the hallway is the lay parson's bench on which visitors used to sit while waiting their turn to go up and visit the ailing Whitman, who was lucid and creative even after he was paralyzed by a stroke. On the wall behind it is the large brown piece of paper on which his attending physician wrote the death notice for throngs of people who waited outside for the news. It states that Walt was conscious until the end.

The spacious bedroom where he spent several years looks as if it has been tidied up by a compulsive housekeeper after his departure. The narrow wooden bed in which he died is neatly made. Alongside it is a photograph of the room when Whitman lived here— cluttered and strewn with papers. Often he worked sitting up in bed, but when he tired of that position he worked at a small table set up between the front windows or in an adjoining bedroom. In a back corner is the special pigeonholed cabinet he had made to organize and store his papers. After recording his conversations with Whitman, Horace Traubel used to file them in the holes there. Other objects of interest are the knapsack in which he carried *Leaves of Grass* as he peddled it around various neighborhoods, and the large circular tin bathtub in which his male nurse used to bathe him.

His nurse Warren Fitzgerald, who attended him for the last two and a half years, and was paid by a group of Whitman's friends, had the small adjoining bedroom. Mark Twain and John Greenleaf Whittier also donated money to buy him a horse and carriage so that he could leave the house and go for rides into the country.

A group of young admirers arranged a large birthday party for Whitman in the parlor on May 31, 1891, when he was 72. Tables were set up in both parlors for the occasion, and the catered dinner lasted for three hours. Liz Perry, one friend who attended, said that Whitman spent most of his time munching on bread dipped in champagne and talked of death. He died ten months later on March 26, 1892.

At **Harleigh Cemetery** (from Walt Whitman House go E on Mickle St. for several blocks and then turn S onto Haddon Ave. Cemetery is at 1640 Haddon Ave.), Whitman's tomb, with its door symbolically ajar, is built into the side of a hill not far from the main gate. In 1890, when the cemetery presented him with a plot of his choice, he designed a much more grandiose structure, which later had to be scaled down, since the funds which his friends supplied were limited. After his death his parents and some of his brothers and sisters were brought here from Long Island to be buried.

The **Walt Whitman International Poetry Center** (Second and Cooper Streets), located nearby in a Grecian style building which was formerly a branch of the Camden Public Library, has a schedule of daily and weekend poetry readings, many by well-known published poets.

New Brunswick

The **Joyce Kilmer Birthplace** (17 Joyce Kilmer Ave.), long a popular New Jersey literary shrine, was until recently open to the public on a regular basis. The mustard and green frame house is now enclosed behind a barbed wire fence and is in disrepair, though tenants live in the back half.

Though often remembered only for his poem "Trees," Kilmer was a featured interviewer and book reviewer and the author of six books of essays and poems when he died on a battlefield in France in 1918. Locally he was mourned as a young teacher who had gone to war and wrote a touching poem, "Trees," in honor of his favorite tree back home, moments before he died. Each Arbor Day celebrations are held under the three-hundred-year-old Joyce Kilmer Oak, thought to be the inspiration for the poem, on the Rutgers University campus. In the 1930s, when interest in Kilmer was at its peak, some admirers had elaborate plans to move the house to the middle of a park they were going to create nearby. The project never became a reality, but there are many streets and businesses named after him.

Princeton

(Street map available at Chamber of Commerce, Nassau St.) A number of houses and buildings in this town have literary associations. Though the houses are privately owned and not open to the public, it is possible to walk or drive to them by following a street map. Countless authors have been writers-in-residence here or have taught at the various halls on campus.

Philip Freneau attended Princeton in the late 1700s and wrote many of his early poems during his undergraduate years. He collaborated with Hugh Henry Brackenridge and James Madison on a satire of the British; they read the poem together at an assembly in **Nassau Hall** (directly across from Palmer Square on Nassau Street), the spot where the British surrendered after the Battle of Princeton.

Many writers got their start with the *Nassau Literary Magazine,* which still has its office in **East Witherspoon Hall** (behind Nassau Hall in the middle of the campus). Booth Tarkington was an editor of that magazine while also running a coffee house on the order of the eighteenth-century literary gathering place. The group grew into the Princeton Triangle Club. He wrote the club's first production, *The Honorable Julius Caesar* and became its producer, set designer, and musical director; he even acted a small part.

Upton Sinclair came to Princeton in 1903 to write a trilogy of Civil War novels, and set himself up in two tents on a ridge three miles north of town. Here he isolated himself, researching and writing. Once a week a buggy came to take him in to the Princeton University Library, now the **Firestone Library,** where he would exchange one set of books for another. When *Manassas* was completed he built a little cabin, with tar-paper roof and potbelly stove, to live in over the winter. After the royalties from his books became more generous he was able to buy a sixty-acre farm at the junction of Province Line Road and Ridge View Road northwest of town. He put the cabin on a farmer's wagon, set it up near the house as a study and retreat, and used it while writing *The Jungle,* which soon began to appear as a serial.

F. Scott Fitzgerald had already published several short stories when he came to Princeton as a freshman in 1913. During his first year, he lived at **15 University Place** (south of Nassau Street across from Palmer Square), and the next year at **107 Patton Hall Tower.** He kept very active writing scripts for the Triangle Club and in 1916 collaborated with Edmund Wilson on *The Evil Eye.* Before leaving Princeton for the Army in November 1917, he contributed to the *Nassau Literary Magazine* and the *Princeton Tiger,* and began working on a novel which eventually became *This Side of Paradise.* The university's **Firestone Library** has a comprehensive collection of Fitzgerald's manuscripts and correspondence.

Thornton Wilder did most of his work of *The Cabala* while teaching at the nearby Lawrenceville School. After he came to Princeton for an M.A. in modern languages, he began *The Bridge of San Luis Rey* and wrote on the top floor of the **Princeton Graduate College** on College Road, which can be reached by going southwest on Mercer Street as it branches off from Nassau Street and then south two blocks on Alexander. He said the idea for the book came to him one day as he walked from the Graduate College to the center of town. During most of his years at Lawrenceville and Princeton he spent evenings poring over dusty books in the basement of the old Princeton University Library.

When Thomas Mann had a lectureship at Princeton from 1938 to 1941 he lived at **65 Stockton Avenue,** now the home of the Aquinas Foundation. During that time he devoted himself to his writing and finished several major works, among them the final book of the *Joseph and His Brothers* tetralogy.

T. S. Eliot lived nearby in a white frame house at **14 Alexander Street** in 1948 and 1949 while he was at the Institute for Advanced Study (Alexander Street runs north and south and can be reached by taking Mercer Street fron Nassau Street and then cutting down Alexander). *The Cocktail Party* was written in Princeton in Room 307 of **Fuld Hall,** the headquarters of the Institute.

William Faulkner often visited the home of his editor Saxe Commins at **85 Elm Road** (Elm Road runs north and south on the western outskirts of Princeton and can be reached by going west on Nassau Street and turning right on Elm Road after Nassau becomes Stockton). The house became a literary haven, with Faulkner often staying for extended periods of time. While working under Commins's guidance, he rewrote *The Town* and *The Mansion.*

There are countless other writers who lived in Princeton for short periods of time. English poet Alfred Noyes wrote a number of his American poems in a study at **120 Broadmead** (Broadmead is a two-block street which can be reached by taking Princeton Avenue south from Nassau Street). In 1952–53 R. P. Blackmur lived in an apartment building at **12 Princeton Avenue** with Saul Bellow, who was a Creative Writing Fellow. During that year Bellow finished *The Adventures of Augie March.* Philip Roth lived at **232 Bayard Lane** (north of Nassau Street just west of Palmer Square). Perhaps the most popular literary site in Princeton is **Linebrook,** the Victorian-style house which John O'Hara built at the intersection of Pretty Brook Road and Province Line Road after his previous residence at 20 College Road West was destroyed by fire in 1960. Many of his later works were written at Linebrook.

McCarter Theater (on University Place) is one of the leading regional arts centers in the country. Each season it presents new plays, classics, and some of the lesser-known plays of major playwrights.

NEW YORK

Austerlitz

Steepletop (off State Route 22, 5 mi. S of NYS Thruway. Ask directions in Austerlitz. Write for appointment), home of Pulitzer Prize-winning poet Edna St. Vincent Millay until her death in 1950, is now being developed into the Millay Colony for the Arts. When she died, "Vincent," as she was popularly known, left her entire estate to develop this wilderness retreat so that other artists could enjoy the peace and tranquillity she had found there.

In 1925 Vincent and her husband, Eugen Boissevain, bought the seven hundred acres of wooded farmland on the western slopes of the Berkshires and with the help of workmen put one of the farms in order, restoring berry patches and fruit orchards, settling in the animals, and adding a few additions to the existing buildings. They often stayed here snowbound for weeks in the winter, and at other times took off on extensive trips to New Mexico, Europe, the Caribbean Islands, Florida, or Manhattan. Eugen, who always maintained that Vincent was a poet rather than a housewife, took care of everything in the house and on the farm. Writer Vincent Sheean

described their life there in his short biography *The Indigo Bunting.*
In 1973, her sister Norma, who as of this writing still lives in the
farmhouse, turned the property over to the Colony. Since that
time barns have been made into dormitories and studio spaces and
a few new buildings have been built in the surrounding oods and
fields without intruding on the natural setting.

The main house, which will eventually be used as the main hall
of the Colony, is a white frame building that stands across the road
from the barns among thick, crowding trees, and was home base
for Vincent and her husband during the many years they lived here.
Two rooms especially reflect her personality and lifestyle. One was
her poetry room upstairs. The other was the simply but comfortably
decorated living room where she pursued two of her main passions,
birds and music. She would sit for hours in her favorite chair by
the living room window to study and feed the birds and could give
comprehensive accounts of the habits of the many species that came
here. One of her prized possessions was a worn-out copy of Audubon's
Birds of America, in which she constantly made notes.

Since her childhood in Camden, Maine (see entry), she had spent
part of each day observing the birds, learning how they nested, how
they lived, and what their songs were. The purple finch, the rose-
breasted grosbeak, and the indigo bunting came frequently. She
also pursued her hobby at their fifty-acre Ragged Island in Maine,
where she spent hours each day swimming among the rocky ledges
of the sea.

There were two pianos in that room also, and after a period of
writing or birdwatching, she often enjoyed playing. At times she
and Eugen played together and in quartets made up of others from
the area. They also gave concerts for guests.

Upstairs in this house was the sanctuary which few were permitted
to enter, the library which was often referred to as the "poetry room."
Here was an extensive collection of outstanding poems written in
English. Vincent had a thorough knowledge of many poets and did
not limit herself to one type. She had books containing works of
Petrarch, Dante, Racine, Shakespeare, Goethe, and many others,
and she could quote endlessly from them for long periods of time.
Her reading and the bird songs were no doubt a storehouse on which
she drew for her own writing. On the walls there were a portrait of

her favorite American poet, Robinson Jeffers, a pencil sketch of Shelley, and several sailing charts of Penobscot Bay. Prominently displayed was a large sign with one word: *Silence.*

Vincent often recited poetry for guests, who came to Steepletop only by invitation or advance notice. They were often entertained at the rustic bar and swimming pool which she and her husband built into the hillside near the house. The spring-fed pool is built from the foundation of an old barn, and the bar and stools from sections of its sides. Both the pool and the lounging area are covered by a complex interweaving of vines and trees. Just down from the pool in the beautiful grass and amphitheater surrounded by a semi-circle of cedar trees they often put on dramatic productions, including some of her own plays.

Vincent's small cabin-studio stands in the woods immediately beyond the house. It is as she left it, decorated with a simple desk and several chairs. Farther on are fields and then the remains of the tennis courts where she and her husband played and held tournaments if there were enough houseguests. At times they were known to have large house parties which lasted for several days.

Vincent died of an apparent heart attack one evening in 1950, a year after the death of her husband. She had been up correcting proofs for a review until dawn when she slumped over on the steps halfway between the bird room and the poetry room. After a small private service with friends playing music and reading poetry, her ashes were buried on the grounds next to her husband's. Their graves, and her mother's, are off in the woods in an area now much overgrown. Her mother's grave is marked with a stone, while the ashes of Edna and Eugen are under plaques.

Cooperstown

The **Fenimore House,** part of the New York State Historical Society
Complex (1 mi. N of town on State Route 80. Open daily; May-Oct.
9-5, July and Aug. 9-9, Nov.-Apr. 9-5; closed Mon. in winter and
Thanks., Dec. 25, Jan. 1. Adm. charged), a red brick mansion built
in 1932 on the site of the simple cottage where James Fenimore
Cooper lived for three years, has one room devoted to Cooper
memorabilia. A sketch of the little cottage and a painting of the
family mansion, Otsego Hall, destroyed by fire in 1853, hang there.
In addition there are paintings depicting a number of scenes from
Cooper's novels: by James William Glass from *The Prairie;* by
John Quidor from *The Pioneers;* by Thomas Cole from *The Last
of the Mohicans;* and by Frederick Edwin Church from *The Spy.*
In a display case on his father's desk is an original letter which
Cooper wrote to his agent from Paris asking him to deposit money
in his New York account. Other items include his wife's copy of
The Last of The Mohicans, a portrait of Cooper's mother, a sculpture of Cooper himself, done in 1828 by David d'Angers, and William
Cooper's land book, a manuscript map of the wilderness area giving
an early plan for Cooperstown. The historical society also has artifacts of Cooper's which can be seen by special arrangement. (The
remainder of the museum is devoted to American and folk art,
including paintings of early life in Syracuse, Utica, and other area
cities.)
   William Cooper, the novelist's father, first came to the area in
1786 and bought forty thousand acres of land. He then laid out
the site of Cooperstown, called Foot of the Lake until 1791, when
it became the county seat. After building a store for the pioneers
he set out to plan the streets, and then built himself his first home,
which was called The Manor. It was finished in 1788. Two years

later he brought his family, including fourteen-month-old James Fenimore, their servants, and their belongings from Burlington, New Jersey. The Manor was a plain two-story frame house with two wings and a back building. It stood facing Main Street and Otsego Lake and later stood directly in front of the much more elaborate Otsego Hall, built in 1798 as the Coopers' permanent home. Otsego Hall was an exact copy of the Van Rensselaer Manor House in Albany.

Many of the area's geographic features appear in the *Leatherstocking Tales,* which give a vivid description of frontier Cooperstown. Lake Otsego, meaning a place of friendly meeting of Indian warriors, was often referred to as Glimmerglass. Mount Vision, a hill southwest of the town, was then covered with growth so dense that a person had to climb a tree to get a glimpse of the lake from there. Then there was Council Rock, just to the west of the point where the lake empties south into the Susquehanna River. That marked the spot where Deerslayer met Chingachgook, "the great Serpent of the Delawares." The opening chapter of *The Deerslayer* describes the wild country there.

Cooper turned to his childhood in *The Pioneers,* which he said was written solely to please himself. Natty Bumppo, sometimes called Leatherstocking, made his first appearance in that novel; he lived in a cave just south of Cooper's Chalet Farm on the east side of the lake. Both the cave and the farm are marked by roadside plaques. Natty, who appeared in all five *Leatherstocking Tales,* is thought to have been patterned after an old hunter named Shipman who often came to the Coopers' door during the early years of the colony and offered game to the family. The children were especially attracted to him. Judge Temple is said to be a faint sketch of Cooper's father. The brave old Indian John of the town was the model for Chingachgook, and a Monsieur Le Quoi for the Frenchman. An actual Indian attack on the village in 1794 is the model for a chapter of *The Deerslayer,* and though the incidents were fictitious, the pigeon flights, Natty's cave, which sheltered Elizabeth Temple from the forest fire, and all the picturesque countryside of Glimmerglass were real. The academy, the courthouse, the jail, the inn, and the famous cannon Cricket, which echoed over the hills on holidays, also actually existed.

Otsego Hall, the family mansion, appeared in *The Pioneers* in Cooper's description of the great landlord living among his settlers on property bearing his name. In a description of the hall he called it a "mongrel of the Grecian and Gothic orders and the admiration of all the mountaineers." Cooper had a large library which was the envy of all in town. In one corner of the room was a large screen with pictures of all the places the family had visited in Europe. Here he wrote many of his works on a walnut writing table which had originally been owned by his maternal grandfather in New Jersey.

Though Cooper died at Otsego Hall in 1851, and he and his wife are buried on the grounds of Christ's Church, he did not live here all his life. After his marriage he left for almost twenty years to live in his wife's hometown, Mamaroneck, New York, since she could not stand frontier life. They later returned to live at Otsego Hall, however.

It is ironic that Cooperstown, a village of museums, makes so little of the author who chronicled the settlement of this area. One has to search hard for Cooper associations. On the road which goes around the edge of the lake are historical markers denoting some scenes from Cooper's novels. Just up the road from Fenimore House on the west side is Sutton Island, home of the Deerslayer. Then there is Leatherstocking Falls, Five Mile Point, and near the northern end, Sunken Island. Coming back down the east side are Gravelly Point, Chalet Farm, Natty Bumppo's Cave, and finally, at the foot of the lake, Council Rock.

Elmira

Mark Twain's Study (on the green at Elmira College campus. Park Place, near Washington Ave. Key available at Elmira College switchboard. Open 8:30 A.M.-4:30 P.M., Mon.-Sat.), designed in the shape of a Mississippi riverboat pilothouse, was restored and moved here to these protected surroundings in 1952. The second summer Twain had come to Quarry Farm, his wife's family place in the hills above Elmira, his sister-in-law surprised him with the small one-room study. Twain described it as a cozy nest, "the loveliest study ever, with its peaked roof and eight spacious windows," and said that it sat in complete isolation on the top of the East Hill and commanded a beautiful view of the valley. During the summer of 1874 he wrote most of *Tom Sawyer* there, and in subsequent years worked on *The Adventures of Huckleberry Finn, The Prince and the Pauper, Life on the Mississippi,* and *A Connecticut Yankee in King Arthur's Court.*

The inside of the study, which has windows all around its perimeter, is as it was when Mark Twain last worked there. His typewriter is under glass next to the fireplace. Against the walls are the various chairs he used, depending on his mood, and on one side is his round working table with drawers. Above the fireplace is a large oil painting of Twain, and on the mantel above the windows are a number of portraits and etchings. Missing are the many papers strewn all over the floor. It was his habit to leave the house in the morning and go to his study to work without stopping for lunch, until late in the afternoon. He let sheet upon sheet of manuscript fall to the floor until day's end, when he collected them all and took his day's work down to the house to be read and discussed with the family.

Samuel Clemens first came to Elmira in the summer of 1868 to

visit Charles Langdon, whom he had met the previous year while
on a trip through Egypt and the Holy Land. Some say Twain met
his wife Olivia, Charles's sister, during that first trip here, though
there is more evidence that they met a short time later when Twain
got together with the Langdons in New York City. Sam and Olivia
were engaged the following winter and had a small wedding on
February 2, 1870, at the Langdon homestead, which stood at the
corner of Church and Main Streets. Shortly before their marriage
the two sat together in the front parlor of the house on Main Street
and corrected proofs of the novel *The Innocents Abroad,* which
was largely based on the Middle Eastern trip Twain and Charles
Langdon had taken.

After living for a year and a half in Buffalo, New York, the
Clemenses moved to Hartford, Connecticut, where they built a
permanent home (see Hartford, Connecticut). For the next twenty
years, however, they often returned to spend summers at Quarry
Farm with Mrs. Clemens's older sister, Susan Langdon Crane, and
her family. Three of the four Clemens children were born at the farm.

During the summers Twain was often seen about town clad in his
traditional white linen suit and panama hat. He had many friends
in Elmira who shared his lifelong passion for billiards, and he played
often with the many prominent Elmira men at the Century Club
(now the Masonic Temple), and at the Langdon farm, which, of
course, was equipped with a billiards table. Often he walked the
two and a half miles from Quarry Farm to the center of town, but
at times came on horseback with his children. Since the horses
needed watering after making the long climb back up East Hill to
the farm, the family placed four troughs near the road, and named
each after one of the children. One of the troughs has been moved
to the Elmira College campus and is situated just to the left of the
study there. It is inscribed "Clara L. Clemens, 1874," for his
daughter. Two of the troughs are still at the farm, one along the
road outside the stone wall, and another slightly down the hill from
the house. A fourth is in private hands.

Quarry Farm (up Jerusalem Hill, off Church St. near intersection of State Routes 7 and 17; house stands west of Crane Rd. off
Watercure Hill), privately owned and not open to the public, is
still used as a country house by the Langdon family. Its combination

of Tudor, gingerbread Victorian, and plain New York styles is unusual for the area, yet the embellishments seem typical of the houses in which Mark Twain lived. A porch spanning the entire front of the house overlooks the valley below. Inside are many of the beautiful family antiques which Twain was familiar with when he lived here. His study, which he used last in the summer of 1903, was originally in an orchard behind the housekeeper's cottage.

Rudyard Kipling made a long hot ride to Quarry Farm in a livery hack in the summer of 1889. He had come from Australia, not yet a well-known author, to interview Mark Twain. They remained good friends from then on and in 1907 received honorary degrees together from Oxford University.

Woodlawn Cemetery (1200 Walnut St.) has the graves of Twain and his family. The Langdon plot has a very high headstone marker with stones spaciously laid out on either side. Nearby is the Mark Twain-Gabrilowitsch monument, erected by his daughter Clara Clemens in honor of her father and her first husband, noted musician Ossip Gabrilowitsch, who had asked to be buried at the foot of Mark Twain. The monument had bas-relief portraits of both men.

Twain's grave is in the middle of the sixteen small Langdon graves there, and is marked "Samuel Langhorne Clemens-Mark Twain—Nov. 30, 1835-Apr. 21, 1910." The grave of Olivia and those of their children have inscriptions by him. His wife's reads "In this grave repose the ashes of Olivia Langdon/the beloved and lamented wife of Samuel L. Clemens/who reverently raises this stone to her memory."

Huntington, Long Island

The **Walt Whitman Home** (on State Route 110, about ½ mi. S
of junction with the Jericho Tpke., in Huntington Station), a weather-
beaten saltbox typical of the early 1800s, stands back from Walt
Whitman Road, its fenced-in yard bordered on all sides by develop-
ments. For many years this was considered Whitman's birthplace;
however, recent evidence indicates that he was born at one of the
other family houses nearby. Whitman's ancestors came to Connecticut from England in 1602 and to Huntington soon after. By the
1700s the family farm had become a prosperous enterprise operated
by many slaves. Walt remembered the original homestead which
stood at a point in West Hills where South Road and Old Coast
Road meet. The existing boyhood home was small in comparison.
  Extensive research was done to restore the Walt Whitman Home
to its condition in the early 1800s. Though supported by several
steel braces, the attic beams which Whitman's father erected are
still held together by the original wooden pegs. On the first floor
is the typical Colonial kitchen with an adjoining borning room.
The second floor has been made into a museum of Whitman memorabilia. One room has an extensive exhibit containing facsimiles
of letters and newspapers to represent the three phases of Whitman's
life—his early years on the farms of Long Island, his middle years
in New York and Washington, and his last ten years in Camden, New
Jersey. On the wall is a copy of the letter which Emerson wrote to
Whitman telling him how much he thought of *Leaves of Grass*. A
second room has an extensive library of original works and criticism.
Here also are the schoolmaster's desk which he used at Woodbury,
Long Island, and a number of personal possessions. His "Diary of
the War" is blown up in large print on the wall.

From the windows on this floor is a view west to the more secluded roads leading up to Jaynes Hill. Admirers of Whitman's poetry can come to this area and drive around the countryside once owned by his ancestors; he referred to this section of Long Island as the "fish-shaped Paumonok where I was born." The fields, woods, and hills Whitman rambled through can be envisioned by taking a ride up to the 420-foot Jaynes Hill in Suffolk County Park, which Whitman biographers claim as the actual setting for *Leaves of Grass.*

Jaynes Hill can be reached by going up West Hills Road across the street from the Whitman house and going left. Past the summit of the hill, which is the highest point on Long Island, and where a rock memorial has been dedicated to Whitman, West Hills Road winds north past a number of houses which have been in the Whitman family at one time or another. All are privately owned now, and not open to the public. Near the first bend on West Hills Road, just before Chichester Road, are the Whitman-Place houses which were owned by Whitman's great-grandfather. The old barn there dates back to 1700 and the house built in 1810 is one mentioned by Whitman. Just past the intersection of West Hills and Chichester Roads are more houses which were in the family. The Whitman-Rome House has the Whitman family burial ground behind it up on a hill.

West on Chichester Road almost at the intersection with Sweet Hollow Road is the old Peace and Plenty Inn, which was the center of social life in Whitman's time. The schoolhouse and the fairylike mountain mist spring that enchanted Whitman as a child were also on this road. The Colyer House, which Whitman often spoke of visiting, is past the western end of Chichester Road at the corner of High Hold Drive and Hartman Hill Road. This was built by his carpenter grandfather. Other sites connected with Whitman are the Long Swamp School House, which stood on the grounds of the present South Huntington Public Library at Depot and Maplewood Roads just north of Jericho Turnpike, and the building that housed the offices of the *Long Islander,* which Whitman founded in 1838, at 313 Main Street in Huntington. The soil and the sea were so much a part of him that during his last years in Camden, when he was no longer able to travel, he urged two English visitors to make a pilgrimage to Long Island and see the sources of his inspiration.

Though Whitman's parents moved the family to Brooklyn when Walt was four, he spent a lot of time with relatives here. As a young boy he made weekly trips to market in Brooklyn and rode back and forth between the various family farmhouses. In addition to the endless round of activities that went with farm life, there was the sea. Sometimes he would follow a brook which led from his grandfather's farm down through the woods to the point where it led into the harbor. He also remembered stories of British occupation and harassment. At twelve, Walt was forced to quit school and work for a small building business which his father had started. When that failed, he worked in a law office and then began writing for the *Long Island Patriot* and several other newspapers, all the time reading voraciously and writing poetry.

When Walt was seventeen he became a country schoolteacher on Long Island, living with various families for short periods of time. While teaching he became active in the community and took part in the local debating society. Some accounts indicate that he was well liked as a teacher, though many report that he had his students write a lot while he sat up at the front desk working on his own poetry.

After teaching at Smithtown during the fall and winter of 1837–38, he started his own newspaper, the *Long Islander*. At that time, the main section of Huntington consisted of the newspaper office, a few houses, and several shops. Walt served as editor, writer, and printer of the paper and slept upstairs over the shop, living very sparsely with only the bare necessities. Some of his subscribers paid him with vegetables and firewood. In the evenings, the youth of Huntington would gather downstairs to listen to Walt read poetry and tell stories. He spent a lot of time strolling throughout the villages and farms, visiting the old whaling center at Cold Spring Harbor and wandering around the old burial ground which the British occupied during the Revolution. He was an important figure in the country village of Huntington. About a year later he became restless, sold the paper, and moved to Brooklyn. Little mention was made of Whitman after he left. In fact, when *Leaves of Grass* came out in 1855 the editor of the *Long Islander* wrote a scathing review of it. Gradually, as Whitman gained stature in the literary world, the paper began to sing his praises, and in 1938, on the one hundredth birthday of its founding, the editors of the paper ran a series of articles in his honor.

For a year or two after leaving Huntington, Whitman wrote for various papers and turned his hand again to teaching for a while at Little Bayside. In the summer of 1840 he taught in a small school at Woodbury, not far from his grandfather's farm. From there he went on to teach in Whitestone during the winter and spring of 1841. He then moved to various boarding places in lower Manhattan and, after working a few years as compositor, free-lance writer, and overseer of his family's properties, became editor of the *Brooklyn Daily Eagle* at twenty-seven. Following that post he held various clerkships in Washington before leaving for Camden, New Jersey (see entry), where he spent the last ten years of his life.

Kinderhook

The **Luycas Van Alen House** (on State Route 9H, 2 mi. S of US 9. Open 10:30 A.M.-4:30 P.M. Tues.-Sat., Memorial Day-Labor Day; after Labor Day-Oct., Sat. only; Sun. all seasons from 1:30 P.M. Closed rest of yr. Adm. charged) was for many years considered the setting for Washington Irving's story, "The Legend of Sleepy Hollow." Local tradition suggested that the Luycas Van Alen family and others in the immediate vicinity were prototypes for characters in the story. Ichabod Crane is said to have been Jesse Merwin, the schoolmaster in the house across the road. Brom Bones or Abraham Van Brunt is said to have been patterned on Abraham Van Alytyne of a nearby farm, and the Headless Horseman after the Hessian soldiers who camped in Kinderhook after Burgoyne's defeat at Saratoga. In truth, however, there is no historical evidence that Irving knew the people of the house. The connection seems to have been suggested by someone in the nineteenth century who was a guest of the Van Alens when Irving was a houseguest and tutor at the nearby Van Ness household, which later became President Martin Van Buren's home, Lindenwald. The curators now emphasize the historic value of the Van Alen house rather than its literary associations.

Perhaps one reason the link between this house and Irving's work was so strong is that the interior reflects such a typical Dutch domestic setting that it would be easy to imagine one of Irving's early works taking place here. In actuality, however, it does not really fit the specific description of the Dutch house in "The Legend of Sleepy Hollow," which resembles more of a lower Hudson Valley style. The Van Alen House resembles the Dutch homes of the Albany area more closely. The three downstairs rooms have large open fireplaces, and are decorated with imported Dutch antiques, oil paintings, and distinctive Hudson Valley chairs and tables dating back to about 1760. The more formal first, or "best," room was reserved for guests and family ceremonies such as baptisms, weddings, and funerals. The second was the large kitchen and borning room and the third was the everyday family parlor or work area.

Set back from the road above a pond, the house, with its Dutch shutters and benches beside the front door, is easily distinguishable. It is one of hundreds of gabled Dutch houses which once dotted the countryside at the northern end of the valley. Though several others still stand, this is the only one restored to its original condition. This type of construction, with its characteristic gables extending up over the roof, was used in the region until the 1750s, when English styles began to predominate.

South of the house is the school which was built in the 1870s on the site of one across the road where Merwin had taught. It was moved here and restored as a gift shop and reception room. On the walls are items relating to the history of the Van Alen House and the school. Of particular interest is a letter which Martin Van Buren wrote testifying that Jesse Merwin, a teacher at Kinderhook School District No. One, actually inspired the character of Ichabod Crane. Van Buren said that Irving had made the acquaintance of Merwin and other Dutch settlers who owned much of the land in the surrounding area.

New Rochelle

The **Thomas Paine Cottage** (at North and Paine Aves. Open 2-5, Tues.-Sun. Free) stands alongside a stream in a small walled-in park just north of town. That plot of land is all that remains of the three hundred acres Paine had been given by the State of New York in recognition of the part that his widely distributed pamphlet "Common Sense" had played in the Revolution.

He originally built the small saltbox on high ground (about a quarter of a mile from its current spot) when he returned from France in 1804 to find that the original farmhouse had been destroyed by fire. It was here, in August 1805, that he wrote his last pamphlet—about constitutional reform in Pennsylvania. The house is now tastefully restored as a museum of New Rochelle and Huguenot history. Each room is filled with fine furniture, etchings, and paintings from families in the area.

Over the front desk in the reception room is an oil portrait of Paine done by a local artist. The rear room of the first floor is known as the Paine Room. On Christmas Eve, 1805, an attempt was made to assassinate Paine by firing at him through the window here. (That incident prompted him to move back to New York City.) Aside from the two chairs which Paine used when he boarded at Bayeau's Tavern, which stood nearby on North Avenue, there is only one real Paine possession in the place—the stove in the middle of the house. It was presented to him by Ben Franklin and is one of the few Franklin stoves extant. When Paine lived here he had few furnishings except for the stove and the straw mattress he slept on.

On the wall alongside the main road a square stone marks the approximate site of Paine's grave. He was buried at that spot just south of the large statue in 1809 after his death in New York City.

According to one local legend, the body was removed in 1819 and taken back to England. On the grave marker are several quotations from John Adams: "Without the pen of Paine the sword of Washington would have been wielded in vain" and "History is to ascribe the American Revolution to Paine." The small building south of the house is the Sophia Brewster schoolhouse, dating back to the 1830s. It was moved here from another spot in New Rochelle.

New York City

Since it would be impossible to cover all of New York City's literary sites, those still standing and those which are part of the past, this section is organized into walking tours of areas where a number of sites still exist. Please see *Literary New York* by Susan Edmiston and Linda D. Cirino for a fuller discussion of New York's literary history. Also, a number of other guidebooks to New York landmarks and historical districts describe these areas in general. Maps and pamphlets are available both at the New York Convention and Visitor's Bureau (90 E. 42 St.) and at the Times Square Information Center.

South of City Hall Park: When Herman Melville was born at **6 Pearl Street** in 1819 this area of Manhattan, now largely dominated by banks and insurance companies, was quite open, and one could look across Battery Park to the harbor. A plaque marking his birthplace is on the north side of a tall office building near the corner of Pearl and State Streets just opposite the Manufacturers Hanover Trust Company.

Trinity Church (Broadway at Wall Street) has the graves of Charlotte Temple and many famous New Yorkers. William Bradford's grave is to the north of the entrance just opposite the north wing of the church. His pithy epitaph tells us that he was born in Leicester, England, in 1663, was the first printer in the colonies, an exponent of freedom of the press, and established the historic point of libel. In 1710 he published America's first Book of Common Prayer and in 1725 the country's first newspaper, the *New York Gazette*. Near the front of the graveyard, just inside the wrought-iron fence, is the supposed grave of Charlotte Temple, heroine of an unhappy love affair during the Revolution. According to the story Susanna Rowson told in her two-volume *Charlotte Temple,* the young English girl came to America and was seduced by an officer who left her with child. She died in 1776. Her dark stone is flush with the ground and all the letters have been worn off. The words "Charlotte Temple" have been recarved. Trinity Church actually has no record of her burial there.

Near the entrance to the south side graveyard is a large memorial to Alexander Hamilton, commemorating him as Washington's aide, founder of the Bank of New York, and one of the framers of the Constitution. He died from a gunshot wound he received in a duel with Aaron Burr on July 12, 1804.

The site of William Bradford's *New York Gazette* is at the **corner of Stone, Hanover, and William Streets.** A plaque on the south side of the Cotton Exchange there marks the site where Bradford was appointed Public Printer in 1698. He issued the first *New York Gazette* on November 8, 1725. **Federal Hall National Memorial** (Wall and Nassau Streets) has a large exhibit on John Peter Zenger, whose acquittal in 1735 on charges of seditious libel was a victory for the principle of freedom of the press.

Washington Irving was born at **131 William Street,** and at the **northwest corner of Ann and William Streets** is a plaque marking the site of his home during the time he was writing *Knickerbocker's History of New York.* Irving was the first to call New York "Gotham."

William Cullen Bryant and James Fenimore Cooper also lived in lower Manhattan when it was still fashionable, and Walt Whitman lived in various downtown rooming houses in his early twenties while he worked as a compositor, free-lance writer, and editor for various papers. He describes Manhattan in several poems.

Brooklyn Bridge has been the subject of a number of works, among them Hart Crane's poem "The Bridge" and Marianne Moore's poem, "Brooklyn Bridge."

Washington Square, North: The heart of literary Greenwich Village is, of course, **Washington Square.** The park itself—originally a potter's field that became chic after it was made into a park and parade ground in 1828—has always been a gathering place. This was true when the wealthy began to build homes in the early nineteenth century, during its Bohemian days, and for the generation after World War II; and it is still true today to some extent.

These blocks were once Henry James and Edith Wharton country. On Washington Square North the row of classic brick houses east of Fifth Avenue, with their granite trim, wrought-iron fences, and marble steps are a scene out of Edith Wharton's *The Age of Innocence* or Henry James's *Washington Square.* Edith Wharton lived for a time at **No. 7** and James used to come here often to visit his grandmother who lived at **No. 19 Washington Square North** (no longer standing). James was born on Washington Place, east of Greene Street, where a New York University building now stands, and a plaque has been placed on a New York University building west of Greene Street. (James also lived at 11 Fifth Avenue and 57 West 14th Street.)

The block behind Washington Square North, east of Fifth Avenue, is **Washington Mews.** The small white houses which face each other on the cobblestone street were once the stables for the houses on the Square. John Dos Passos lived for a time in the studio building between No. 14 and 15, and Sherwood Anderson often stayed at No. 54. **Cedar Tavern** (82 University Place, formerly at 24 University Place), originally a hangout for abstract painters, became a literary gathering place after Allen Ginsberg, Gregory Corso, Jack Kerouac, and others made it popular.

On Fifth Avenue, just north of the Square, literary life revolved around the Brevoort Hotel that once stood at the northeast corner of Fifth Avenue and 8th Street. In 1936 James T. Farrell still considered it the place to stay, but it was torn down after World War II. Other demolished buildings on Fifth Avenue include No. 1, where Sara Teasdale committed suicide in 1933; No. 11, where Henry James lived; No. 16, where Bret Harte stayed in 1870; No. 21,

Mark Twain's brownstone mansion; No. 23, where Mabel Dodge held her salons; No. 35, where Willa Cather lived in a hotel.

At **14 West 10th Street,** a plaque marks the house where Mark Twain lived for a while. It is a four-story red brick with a basement entrance, stone embellishments, and very large windows. At **54 West 10th Street** is the six-story red brick house with basement entrance where Hart Crane lived. Marianne Moore lived in a nine-story brown brick apartment building at **35 West 9th Street.** She donated her entire parlor to the Rosenbach Foundation Museum in Philadelphia, where it is now on display. Still standing is the **Salmagundi Club** (47 Fifth Avenue at 11th Street), in an elegant brownstone, founded in 1871 as a social club for artists and writers. It takes its name from a series of satirical pamphlets which Washington Irving and others wrote about New York. Around the corner at **21 East 11th Street** is the red brick house with wrought-iron trim where Henry James often stayed when he came back to New York from visits to England. It was owned by Edith Wharton's sister-in-law Mary Cadwalader Jones, who entertained many writers and artists. Just east at **No. 25** was the house where Hart Crane stayed as a boarder. Two blocks northwest are two houses where influential literary magazines of the twenties were published. *The Dial* came out of **152 West 13th Street,** the light stone walk-up with fancy wrought-iron trim and carved door, and *The Liberator* from the plainer red brick building with courtyard at **No. 138.**

Washington Square, South: Washington Square South was once lined with row houses similar to those still lining the north side of the park; as the aristocrats moved out, these became boardinghouses occupied by writers such as Theodore Dreiser, O. Henry, Eugene O'Neill, Stephen Crane, and many others. The elaborately embellished sand-colored brick building, **Judson Hall** (51 Washington Square South), one of New York University's buildings, earlier in the century was a hotel where writers and artists stayed. A block south via Sullivan Street is **85 West 3rd Street,** a charming little four-story brick house with arched doors and ironwork at the windows. Edgar Allan Poe lived here for a time.

MacDougal Street, where Eugene O'Neill got the Provincetown Players (133 MacDougal) started in the 1920s, runs parallel to Sullivan Street. The Liberal Club used to meet at 133 MacDougal. Many of the group were theater people who eventually founded the Theatre Guild, and writers such as Sherwood Anderson and Vachel Lindsay. The bars and coffee houses, many of which are now gone, were gathering places for the Beats. Between Sullivan and MacDougal, at **172 Bleecker Street,** is the building where James Agee lived for a time. He had a large apartment on the top floor with wide windows. **East on Bleecker Street,** between West Broadway and Thompson Street, is a former hotel where Theodore Dreiser settled in 1895. Across the street at **No. 145** is the four-story walk-up which James Fenimore Cooper once occupied.

West of Washington Square: Marta's Restaurant (in basement of 75 Washington Place) was a gathering place for writers including John Dos Passos in the 1920s. Across the street, at **No. 82,** is the six-story apartment building with stone and wrought-iron trim where Willa Cather and, later, Richard Wright lived. At **238 West 4th Street** is the gray brick five-story walk-up with many fire escapes on the front where Edward Albee wrote *The Zoo Story.* Sinclair Lewis lived in the four-story gray and white house at **69 Charles Street,** and Hart Crane at **79 Charles Street.** Thomas Wolfe lived two blocks away at **263 West 11th Street.** This four-story red brick walk-up with black trim appears in his novel *You Can't Go Home Again.* The **White Horse Tavern** (567 Hudson Street) was popular with writers during the fifties.

Southwest of Washington Square is St. Luke's Place (between Seventh Avenue South and Hudson Street), with a cluster of Italian-style brownstones with literary associations. In the twenties Sherwood Anderson lived in the fancy red brick one, **No. 12.** Marianne Moore lived at **No. 14,** the ivy-covered house with a stone bottom and brick top. Theodore Dreiser rented the first floor of **No. 16.** At **75½ Bedford Street** (between Seventh Avenue South and Christopher Street) is the nine-and-a-half-foot-wide house where Edna St. Vincent Millay lived briefly after her marriage to Eugen Boissevain (see Austerlitz, New York).

Chumley's (86 Bedford Street), which carries on its speakeasy tradition by having no sign on the door, has been a literary bar for years, with frequent poetry readings and other events still going on.

Patchin Place is loaded with atmosphere. E. E. Cummings and his wife lived here for years, spending the winters in New York and summers at their New England farm. At one point a city agency tried to evict him because the building did not conform to health codes. The whole affair created such a furor that the mayor had to intervene and make a special exception for him.

East Village: The East Village has been home base for such writers as James Fenimore Cooper, and more recently W. H. Auden, LeRoi Jones (now Amiri Baraka), Allen Ginsberg, and Jack Kerouac. Le Metro Cafe (which was at 149 Second Avenue) and Les Deux Magots (which stood on East 7th Street) were former coffee shops where poets read aloud. LeRoi Jones lived at 27 Cooper Square early in his writing career. At 6 St. Mark's Place is the red brick house that James Fenimore Cooper rented in the 1830s. It now has an addition built on to the first two stories and is covered with fire escapes. Farther east, at 77 St. Mark's Place, is the plain brick house with basement entrance where W. H. Auden spent twenty years.

East and North of Union Square: Between East 14th Street and Gramercy Park, six blocks north, are a number of sites with literary associations. At the corner of Irving Place and East 17th Street, **122 East 17th Street,** a romantic two-story walk-up with fancy ironwork is marked with a bronze plaque which says that Washington Irving lived there. Recent evidence indicates that he never really occupied the house but probably visited often while staying with his nephew at 46 East 21st Street. O. Henry made his home for a time on the next block at **55 Irving Place.** The house and others next to it now have a new brick facade. The front parlor window from which he used to watch the crowds was in the same spot as the large restaurant window is now.

Pete's Tavern (129 East 18th Street), where O. Henry used to

spend many hours, was then Healy's Cafe. The dimly lit interior
with its dark carved walls and furniture is like a scene out of an O.
Henry story. On the walls of the first two rooms are many newspaper articles on O. Henry and his associations here, as well as
numerous photographs. The last room at the back with the brick
walls was originally the old stable.

At **170 Third Avenue** is the former Scheffel Hall (now called
Tuesday's), the beautiful old German beer hall with an elaborately
carved interior O. Henry described in one of his stories. At **241
East 17th Street** is the elegant brownstone where William Dean
Howells lived for a short time. The four-story house with iron
grillwork faces Stuyvesant Park. Howells had earlier lived in a
house at **330 East 17th Street.**

Up on Gramercy Park, at the northern end of Irving Place, is
the **Players Club** (16 Gramercy Park South), which still has a large
literary membership. However, it is kept going today by well-to-do
publishers and authors rather than by struggling writers. The club,
a Gothic Revival five-story brownstone, has a paneled interior
covered with memorabilia from the arts. It has counted among its
members such literary greats as Mark Twain and Booth Tarkington.
The **National Arts Club** (15 Gramercy Park South) has long been
a haven for writers and artists. Today many of them reside in
apartment-studio living spaces behind the Arts Club.

Chelsea: The once-fashionable area of Chelsea has long attracted
writers. Many of them have been long-term guests at the **Hotel
Chelsea** (222 West 23rd Street, between Seventh and Eighth Avenues),
a very elaborate orange Gothic-Victorian building with French
doors and wrought-iron balconies on every floor. A plaque on the
front is dedicated to Dylan Thomas, who "labored last here and
then sailed home to die," and to Thomas Wolfe, who lived in the
hotel during the last few years of his life. Among other writers who
stayed here were Mark Twain, O. Henry, Eugene O'Neill, Edgar
Lee Masters, who wrote the poem "The Hotel Chelsea," and Bren-
dan Behan.

In the next block east, at **165 West 23rd Street,** is the dilapidated brownstone where Stephen Crane lived for a time. North a few blocks on West 25th Street, between Sixth Avenue (Avenue of the Americas) and Broadway, is the block where Edith Wharton lived when she was first married. The elegant brownstones have long since made way for commercial buildings.

The Caledonia Hotel (28 West 26th Street), a seven-story building with an elaborate stone bottom, is the place where O. Henry lived for the last years of his life until his death in 1910.

On 28th Street, between Avenue of the Americas and Broadway, are a few of the elegant houses which lined the streets of Chelsea at the turn of the century. Edith Wharton's brother lived on this block as did the characters in her *The Age of Innocence.* A few old brownstones remain tucked in between parking garages and other large commercial buildings.

Midtown: Farther uptown are a number of large hotels with literary associations. The **Algonquin** (59 West 44th Street), longtime gathering spot for writers, birthplace of *The New Yorker* magazine (it was here, it is said, that Harold Ross won the money for the publishing venture in a card game), and home of the famous Round Table of Dorothy Parker, George S. Kaufman, Alexander Woollcott, Robert Benchley, and others, is still frequented by writers and publishers. Inside, the sitting rooms are elegantly decorated with dark woodwork and plush chairs.

The **Biltmore** (Madison Avenue and 43rd Street) is an elaborate sand-colored building which takes over much of the block. Inside, the atmosphere is Parisian, with elaborate ballrooms, carved ceilings, and many chandeliers. Zelda and F. Scott Fitzgerald spent part of their honeymoon here.

The elegant **St. Regis Hotel** (on Fifth Avenue at 55th Street) has fancy marble trim. Amy Lowell considered this home when she was in New York. New York's most spectacular old hotel is the **Plaza** (Fifth Avenue and Central Park South), with its facade of dormers, balconies, and fancy balustrades. F. Scott Fitzgerald immortalized the Plaza in *The Great Gatsby,* and it has since been declared a national landmark. Just west is the **St. Moritz** (50 Central

Park South), which was once the gathering place for Hemingway and other writers. William Dean Howells also lived in a house on this site.

The **Gotham Book Mart** (41 West 47th Street), founded by Frances Steloff in 1920, has been a gathering place for writers for many years; in the thirties (when the store was located at 51 West 47th Street), lectures by writers were given, as well as publication parties. The store remains the cluttered treasure house it has always been.

The **Pierpont Morgan Library** (29 East 36th Street. Open Tues.-Sat. 10:30-5, Sun. 1-5. Closed Sun. in July, Aug.-Labor Day, and hols. Free) has one of the greatest collections of rare manuscripts and books in the world. The outstanding permanent exhibit includes a Gutenberg Bible, and special exhibits range from medieval illuminated manuscripts to the letters of famous authors.

Farther uptown, at Fifth Avenue and 42nd Street, is the **New York Public Library,** which in addition to its millions of volumes usually has special displays relating to literature and the history of printing, including rare books, autograph manuscripts, and letters of writers.

East Side: Turtle Bay Gardens (48th Street, between Second and Third Avenues), a group of old historic homes, was once farmland. Many literary and theatrical people have lived in the small brownstones with their private garden. Edgar Allan Poe lived for a time during the 1840s at the Miller farmhouse, which stood nearby in the fields at 47th Street and Second Avenue. Soon after, Margaret Fuller lived with the Horace Greeleys in the vicinity of 50th Street. A number of modern writers have lived at **Beekman Place** (runs east of First Avenue between 49th and 51st Streets). The locale has appeared in many works of literature. At **330 East 51st Street** is the small brick house where John Steinbeck lived in the fifties and kept a garden.

On the east side of Central Park from 48th up to 96th Streets are a number of multistory brick apartment houses where novels were written and set. Willa Cather made her home at **570 Park Avenue** (corner of 63rd Street), an early twentieth-century brick apart-

ment building. At **35 East 84th Street,** near the corner of Park
Avenue, Eugene O'Neill had a penthouse apartment late in his life.
He also lived briefly in a plain brick apartment building at 1085
Park Avenue.

West Side: The West Side is much more a blend of commercial
and residential buildings than the East Side. One of the most elaborate old West Side apartment-hotels is the **Ansonia** (at 73rd Street and
Broadway), once the residence of Theodore Dreiser. With its many
terraces and dome on top it looks like a wedding cake from a distance.

The area between the Ansonia and the Columbia University
campus is now totally built up. It is hard to believe that Edgar
Allan Poe spent the summer at an isolated farmhouse at **84th Street**
and West End Avenue. Sinclair Lewis lived several blocks east in
an apartment at **300 Central Park West.**

At **333 Riverside Drive** is the beautiful turn-of-the-century
Beaux Arts-style house where Saul Bellow lived in the fifties. At
380 Riverside Drive (corner of 110th Street) is a tall brick apartment
building which J. D. Salinger used as the setting for his fictional
Glass family.

The **West End Cafe** (2911 Broadway, between 113th and 114th
Streets), now a bar-delicatessen serving the Columbia University
area, was a hangout for beat poets in the late forties when Allen
Ginsberg was a student at Columbia. North of the Columbia campus
at **200 Claremont Avenue** is the red brick apartment building where
F. Scott Fitzgerald lived while struggling to become a writer.

The Bronx: Poe Cottage (2640 Grand Concourse at Kingsbridge
Road in Poe Park. Open Sat. 10-4, Sun. 1-5; weekdays by appt.;
phone 881-8900. Sm. adm. charged), where Edgar Allan Poe, his
ailing wife Virginia, and his mother-in-law and aunt, Mrs. Clemm,
came in 1846, was originally part of the tiny village of Fordham.
They rented a small workman's house from a John Valentine for one
hundred dollars a year. St. John's College, now Fordham University,
which Poe often visited, was nearby, and he could look through
rolling lawns and apple orchards to Long Island Sound in the distance. The cottage originally stood about four hundred feet away
on Kingsbridge Road, but was moved in 1913 when it was dedicated
as a museum and the green around it designated as Poe Park.

When Poe came here he was already famous for his short stories and his long poem "The Raven," published in 1845. But although well known, Poe was abjectly poor. Both Mrs. Clemm and Poe often found it necessary to go to the neighbors for food, and some contemporaries actually remembered Mrs. Clemm walking the streets of the village, basket in hand, begging for the night's supper. In 1847, when Virginia died of tuberculosis in the back bedroom, she had only a thin sheet and a threadbare overcoat of Poe's to cover her.

In Philadelphia Poe had perfected the horror and detective story. Here at Fordham he turned to the theme of death and wrote his well-known poems "Annabel Lee," "Ulalume," and "The Bells," all of which idealize Virginia and reflect the ominousness of the illness they all fought for several years.

The house is sparsely decorated, as it must have been when Poe was here. In the kitchen are a stove, table, and chairs. On the wall in the parlor is a photograph which the Brooklyn Museum created according to Poe's description of the ideal room in his short piece, "The Philosophy of Furniture." Though he had an attic study on the second floor, he probably did most of his writing in this room because it would have been warm and full of light during the day. Poe's rocker, one of the two original pieces in the house, is here. The other is the bed on which Virginia died in the back room. In a display area is a drawing of the way the cottage looked in 1846, and a bust of Poe done in 1909 for the one hundredth anniversary of his birth.

The **Hall of Fame** (part of Bronx Community College Campus, Hall of Fame Terrace, between Sedgwick and University Avenues. Open daily except hols. 10-5. Free) has busts of eighty-nine famous Americans, many of them writers.

The **Wave Hill Mansion** (675 West 252nd Street, at Sycamore Avenue, Riverdale), which commands a magnificent view of the Hudson River, has been the home of Mark Twain, Theodore Roosevelt, and Arturo Toscanini. It is now owned by the Parks Department and is used as an environmental center.

Brooklyn: Many writers have lived in **Brooklyn Heights** at one time or another. Near the end of his life Thomas Paine lived in a house which stood on the corner of **Sands and Fulton Streets.** **Plymouth Church of the Pilgrims** (Orange Street between Henry and Hicks. Open 9-5, Mon.-Fri., Sept.-June, 9-3 in July and Aug. Guided tours after 11 A.M. service) had as its clergyman Harriet Beecher Stowe's brother Henry Ward Beecher, himself a fierce abolitionist. Among the lecturers who spoke there were Charles Dickens, William Makepeace Thackeray, and Ralph Waldo Emerson. The history of Puritanism is portrayed on a series of nineteen windows.

Many old houses on **Columbia Heights** can be seen by looking up from the Promenade. Thomas Wolfe lived at times at both **No. 111** and **No. 101 Columbia Heights,** and **No. 176** was the home of Henry Ward Beecher in the 1850s. Beecher also lived farther back from the bay at **22 Willow Street.** A plaque marks **No. 155 Willow,** where Arthur Miller lived from 1951 to 1956. At nearby **Montague Terrace,** W. H. Auden lived for a time at **No. 1,** Thomas Wolfe at **No. 5,** and Jules Feiffer at **No. 11.** Arthur Miller and Norman Mailer have also lived in a number of other houses in the area.

Brooklyn's most famous nineteenth-century literary resident was Walt Whitman, who lived in Brooklyn as a boy and later returned in the 1840s to be editor of the *Brooklyn Daily Eagle* and then of the *Brooklyn Freeman* (see Huntington, Long Island). Unfortunately, all the buildings Whitman is known to have lived in have been torn down.

North Hills, Long Island

"The Knothole" (in Christopher Morley Park, Searington Rd., just N of L.I. Expressway, Exit 36) is the study Christopher Morley built in the backyard of his home. In his preface to the eleventh edition of *Bartlett's Familiar Quotations,* which he edited in the early 1930s, Morley wrote that he had built himself a pinewood cabin to "consort with the shade of John Bartlett." As a busy columnist for the *Saturday Review* and judge for the Book-of-the-Month Club, he needed a place to spread out his books and papers and write.

At first the study was considered an oddity in this suburban community and a long and complicated fight ensued with the local zoning board, but eventually Morley emerged the victor and "The Knothole," as the building was called, remained in the yard for the rest of his life. Writers such as Clifton Fadiman, Norman Cousins, and the Benéts often came here to discuss books. It has now been moved to a peaceful setting in the midst of Christopher Morley Park, where he often used to walk with his children.

When "The Knothole" is open, visitors can wander in and out, stopping to sit on the built-in window seats to read current papers and books which are left out for browsing. Morley's large desk, with his pipe and inkwell, dominates the scene. In addition to books, letters, documents, and other memorabilia on display, there is an extensive collection of his works. One unique feature is the bathroom, designed by Buckminster Fuller. All of its facilities are molded from one piece of metal and welded intact. When it was installed, it had to be lowered through the roof. In this cabin Morley wrote four novels: *Kitty Foyle, The Trojan Horse, History of an Autumn,* and *The Man Who Made Friends With Himself,* as well as many reviews, poems, and essays.

Saranac Lake

The **Robert Louis Stevenson Memorial Cottage** (11 Stevenson Lane. Follow signs from Saranac Lake Village. Open June 15-Sept. 15, daily except Mon., 9:30 A.M.-noon, 1-4:30 P.M. Closed rest of yr. Adm. charged) was an isolated hunting lodge in 1887 when Stevenson, his recently widowed mother, his wife Fanny, his stepson Lloyd Osbourne, and their Swiss maid Valentine came for a five-month stay. At that time the frame house and barn were in the woods, and the dirt road, now a lane through this residential area on the outskirts of Saranac Lake, was the main thoroughfare to the nearby stagecoach center of Bloomingdale.

When the family came from Scotland to New York in the summer of 1887, the plan was for Stevenson to see publishers and for the family to find a place to settle for a few months of rest and relaxation before taking a steamer to the South Seas. Their first thought had been a health resort in Colorado, but someone recommended that Robert take a rest cure with Dr. Trudeau, the established expert on tuberculosis, who ran a clinic in Saranac Lake. Also, the clear and cold weather would be beneficial for his consumption. The moment Stevenson came to this remote village twenty-seven miles from the Canadian border, he was enchanted by the forests and mountains and described the countryside as an "American Switzerland."

The land was then owned by a family named Baker, who kept a hotel at the bottom of the hill and used the cottage to take in boarders during the hunting and fishing seasons. The Bakers gave over most of the cottage to the Stevenson party and kept several rooms for themselves. The Bakers, along with Valentine, cooked and cared for the family. Though they had household help, life was kept intentionally spartan in the style of a typical hunter's cottage. It was a rather rustic setting, especially for an ailing man used to refined comforts, yet Stevenson seemed intrigued by the natural beauty and bought snowshoes, a huge fur coat, and a hat so that he could spend time walking through the woods and down to the village.

He did, however, write of the unbearable cold. By mid-November the temperature had dropped to twenty-five degrees below zero and they had to contend with frozen clothes and frostbite. There was little heat in the cottage and water had to be carried from the bottom of the hill. One story is that the water froze one morning before Mrs. Baker could pour it from the water jug into the oatmeal pot. Their usual pattern was to have fires lit early in the day, and lie in bed during the morning hours, Stevenson and his stepson Lloyd Osbourne writing and mother Fanny reading and writing letters. By noon the cottage was warm enough so that they could arise for lunch.

Stevenson came here as the famous author of *Treasure Island* and *Dr. Jekyll and Mr. Hyde,* and when he arrived in New York he was sought after by publishers. *Scribner's* magazine gave him a lucrative contract for writing one article a month. Those pieces later proved to be some of his best essays. In addition he collaborated with his stepson Lloyd on "The Wrong Box" and also wrote most of his long tale, *The Master of Ballantrae.* The origins of the story went back eleven years, when he had passed through Ballantrae on a walking tour through Carrick and Galloway, in Scotland. One winter's night in Saranac Lake as he paced back and forth on the veranda in his buffalo-skin overcoat, the story came to him. It was dark and clear and he could smell, as he called it, the "purity of the forest." With the sound of cracking ice down at the river and a light or two far in the distance, he had the isolation he needed to plan out the story.

After he sketched out the first few chapters, *Scribner's* offered him a contract to do the remainder by serialization. However, once he left Saranac Lake he found it difficult to continue and the book wasn't finished until two years later, in Honolulu.

In early spring, when the Stevensons started talking of their trip to the South Seas, the editor of the New York *World* offered them what had been a long-sought-after dream of Stevenson's, an exotic voyage on a chartered yacht to be paid for by monthly letters of their experiences to the American papers. His wife Fanny went ahead to California in April to book the boat and they took off on the cruise, spending time in Hawaii and eventually settling in Samoa where he bought property called Vailima. He died there in 1894.

Stevenson's large bedroom in the Saranac Lake cottage is now a comprehensive museum with a number of display cases containing various memorabilia.

His years in Samoa are represented by a photograph of his funeral, a model of the outrigger he used there, and other personal articles such as address books, writing implements, cards, clothes, and shoes. In addition to many photographs of Stevenson, there are pictures of the houses he lived in around the world. There are also many letters, illustrations from his works, articles, and reviews on display. On one wall is a huge oil painting of him by local artist Mary Lawson.

Several other rooms have Stevenson furniture and possessions. The small den in the back has the desk on which he wrote. At times he also worked sitting up in the small bed with a lapboard or in an invalid chair. On the walls are the original blocks he drew to illustrate the *Chap Books,* and some pictures of his winter here. Upstairs are the rooms where his stepson Lloyd and their maid Valentine lived. The parlor, where the family did most of their entertaining, has the original Victorian furniture. On the mantelpiece are his cigarette burns, which he was notorious for leaving wherever he went. Hanging on the wall is a plaque by Saint-Gaudens, some photographs of Stevenson, and one of his poems. His mother's bedroom next door contains the original bed. On the north side of the house is the porch on which he paced up and down while planning *The Master of Ballantrae.*

Saratoga Springs

Yaddo (off Union Ave.), since 1926 a colony for artists and writers, has its rose gardens and a section of its wooded grounds open to the public. Scaled terraces with oblong beds of roses lead to a rose-covered pergola halfway up the hill to the original Trask mansion, now one of many buildings which have been converted into studios. When they are in bloom the flowers are reflected in a large fountain at the bottom of the hill.

The property originally belonged to New York stockbroker Spencer Trask, who willed his estate as a writer's colony. He designed the gardens as a present for his wife in 1899. Near the fountain is a statue dedicated to the four Trask children, all of whom died in infancy or early childhood. They were responsible for the name Yaddo, which was their pronunciation of the word "shadow."

Among the guests, all of whom are screened and invited by a committee of judges, have been Theodore Roethke, William Carlos Williams, Katherine Anne Porter, Truman Capote, John Cheever, Carson McCullers, Philip Roth, Flannery O'Connor, Jules Feiffer, and Sylvia Plath.

Edgar Allan Poe is often mentioned in connection with Yaddo; however, it was Barhyte's Tavern, which stood on the site before the estate, that he visited. According to local legend he worked on the final draft of "The Raven" in 1842 and finished the poem there in 1843.

Schaghticoke

The **Knickerbocker Mansion** (just W of Fort Schaghticoke. Operated by the Knickerbocker Historical Society. Open May-Sept., daily 2-5; Oct.-Apr. by appt.), recently restored and decorated with period antiques from the area, is often associated with Washington Irving's *Knickerbocker's History of New York* even though there are no records that he ever visited this far north in the Hudson Valley. One local legend maintains that he wrote a portion of the work while seated at a desk in the parlor.

Though he mentions the Knickerbockers of Schaghticoke and the mansion in the introduction and several times throughout the work, those references were not specific, and could have described many Dutch manor houses. Irving was familiar with many Dutch communities, and a character such as Diedrich Knickerbocker, the pretended author of the History, would have been the composite of many persons. In another work Irving described him as a descendant of one of those ancient Dutch families who still remained in villages and neighborhoods in various parts of the country. Certainly this figure with stooped shoulders, knee britches, a three-cornered hat, and cane was as familiar a sight farther south around Tarrytown (scc cntry) as he was north of Albany.

Near the mansion is the cemetery where generations of the family are buried. The grave of Diedrich's prototype, the original Harmen Jansen Knickerbocker, who came to the Albany area from Friesland in northwestern Holland in the 1670s and died around 1716, is marked by a rough boulder.

The Knickerbocker Mansion is built on land owned by the family from 1708 until 1946, and some parts of the interior date back to the early eighteenth century. In 1770 the whole building was reconstructed according to a Flemish design, which included Dutch bricks and mortar, a steep-pitched roof, and a number of quaint carvings. Some of these embellishments have been covered over with nine-teenth-century additions, and the wooden outbuildings and Dutch-style barns disappeared long ago. In 1960 a community-wide effort produced funds to purchase and restore this mansion, thereby saving it from bulldozers. The historical society is still raising money to make further renovations according to the recommendations of architectural historians.

Tarrytown

Sunnyside (on W. Sunnyside Lane, W of US 9, 1 mi. S of Dewey Thrwy. exit 9. Open daily 10 A.M.-5 P.M. Closed Thanks., Dec. 25, Jan. 1. Adm. charged. Exhibits at Visitors' Center), popularly known as the Van Tassel House of "The Legend of Sleepy Hollow," had once been a Dutch farm cottage on the seventeenth-century manor of Dutch merchant prince Frederick Philipse. Irving came across it as he was reacquainting himself with his old Knickerbocker haunts in the Hudson Valley after having spent seventeen years as a diplomat in Europe. With the help of his artist friend George Harvey he transformed the simple structure, which he described as a "common colonial saltbox," into the romantic country house known to many Americans through a widely distributed Currier and Ives lithograph.

For a while Irving commuted from Manhattan to the picturesque Hudson River estate, then called the "Roost." He spent his first winter there in 1836–37 and his Rocky Mountain fur trade volume, *The Adventures of Captain Bonneville,* was the first manuscript to be completed at Sunnyside. That spring he was visited by Louis Napoleon, later Napoleon III. The house was always overflowing with family and guests, who would come for short visits and spend most of their time in the downstairs study engaged in lively conversation. Eventually Irving's older brother Ebenezer moved in for good and Ebenezer's daughters considered Sunnyside their home.

Irving's stay at Sunnyside was abruptly interrupted in 1842 when President Tyler chose him as minister to Madrid. When he returned in 1846 he was 63. He then redesigned the interior and exterior of the house with Dutch and Spanish motifs to make more comfortable quarters for guests and servants. The most unusual part of the reconstruction was the "pagoda," a three-story tower at the back with a slanting roof and bell on top.

In 1848 his publisher, George Putnam, persuaded Irving to revise fifteen volumes of his *Knickerbocker's History of New York*. From then on he worked feverishly on his biography of George Washington. Despite being busy writing in his study during those later years, he often had visitors, and found himself invited out for dinner parties, going up to Saratoga for jaunts, and taking off on long trips to do research for the biography. By 1854 Sunnyside had become so popular that the name of a nearby town was changed from Deerman to Irvington.

William Makepeace Thackeray came to visit in 1855 and wrote to his daughters that the old Irving was tended affectionately by two nieces in a sunny little cottage surrounded by lawns. He said it was rather shabby, with little bits of parlors inside where they were served cake and wine while dogs and ducks trotted about the premises.

During 1858 Irving struggled with the Washington biography as he was slowly being overcome by asthma. Dr. Oliver Wendell Holmes visited him then and sensed the severity of his illness. After a long conversation he noticed how difficult it was for Irving to talk and breathe and prescribed certain palliatives for his chronic shortness of breath and chest pains. Many visitors came, even near the end, some out of simple curiosity and others because they were sincerely interested in conversing with Irving. However, he never complained and rarely refused anyone. He died in the upstairs bedroom on November 28, 1859.

The study, the first room to the right, is exactly as Irving left it, perhaps minus the clutter. Here he worked at the large desk given to him by his publisher, G. P. Putnam. The walls of this cozy room are lined with his personal collection of books; at one end, behind a drape, is the couch on which he napped. During his first ten years at Sunnyside this served as a one-room apartment for him since the rest of the house was often taken up by his older brother and two young nieces. It was after his return from his diplomatic stint in Spain that he added the pagoda tower for servants and overflow guests and built himself a bedroom upstairs. However, the study was always the focal point of the house. He spent almost all his time here, and was easily able to jump up to greet visitors at the front door and usher them in. On either side of the fireplace mantel are original wash drawings by George Cruikshank, illustrator of *Knickerbocker's History of New York* and also Charles Dickens's chief illustrator. Under the seat of the large leather chair near the door, which many visitors must have sunk into when reaching this cozy room, is a large locked drawer into which Irving stuffed the manuscript in progress before answering the door.

Scattered around the house are many fine pieces of furniture and bric-a-brac from Spain and Holland. The influence of those years abroad is evident not only in the decorating but also in the construction of the house: the arched windows, curved entryways, and interesting nooks and crannies he had built in.

A glimpse of Sunnyside as a literary gathering place is seen in the oil painting "Washington Irving and His Literary Friends at Sunnyside," painted after Irving's death by Christian Schussele. These are friends the artist imagined coming to gather around Irving and partake of the warmth and peacefulness which this house was known to have. Among others are Oliver Wendell Holmes, Nathaniel Hawthorne, Ralph Waldo Emerson, William Cullen Bryant, and James Fenimore Cooper.

Irving's bedroom is especially interesting in light of the Dutch and Spanish influence. He had the ceiling carved in European fashion. Next to his bed is a small night table which he used for writing. Placed around the room are his cane, top hat, shaving equipment, foot rest, and a few other items. Nearby is the tiny bedroom of his nephew Pierre Munro Irving, who stayed here for an extended period in 1859 and helped his ailing uncle complete the last volume of his Washington biography. One large bedroom overlooking the river has an enormous Dutch sleigh bed built into the recess of the wall. There is also the foreign language collection he referred to while writing and doing research on Christopher Columbus. Irving, like many other major eighteenth- and nineteenth-century writers, had little formal education. He was tutored by his fiancée's father and taught himself French, Spanish, and Dutch.

The other buildings of the estate, the outhouse, root cellar, and icehouse, have been restored using documentary sources. At the visitors' bureau, near the front entrance, there is a permanent exhibit with original letters, manuscripts, photographs, and paintings. Included is a watercolor by George Butler picturing Irving's nurse-maid introducing him to Washington when he was ten. From that time on he was one of Washington's most ardent followers. Also displayed are an 1825 note from an English publisher who approached Irving about doing the biography of Washington, and sections from the manuscript of the last volume, which Irving wrote during his race with death in April 1859. A letter written around that time shows his determination to finish the volume despite his weakened condition. There are also examples of critical approval he received from such nineteenth-century historians as Bancroft, Motley, and Prescott.

Sleepy Hollow Cemetery (North Tarrytown. Main entrance N of the Old Dutch Church. Follow markers to Irving family plot) has the grave of Washington Irving. The Irving plot, about fifty feet square, is surrounded by an iron fence. His modest stone, slightly higher than those of the fifty-odd Irving family members surrounding it, is marked "Washington Irving, born April 3, 1783, died November 28, 1859." The Old Dutch Church just south of the cemetery was immortalized in many of his works.

Troy

(Lansingburgh Section): Herman Melville's home (left side of large wooden house at corner of First Ave. and 114th St.), now privately owned, is seldom mentioned in accounts of his life even though he wrote his first two novels there. A group of Melville admirers is trying to create interest in restoring the house and opening it to visitors. Melville lived here from the spring of 1838 to the spring of 1839, and came back after his two-year voyage to the South Seas to write *Typee* (1846), and *Omoo* (1847). His mother had moved the family from Albany to this house "very pleasantly situated on the bank of the Hudson" since living expenses were less than in the city. At that time Lansingburgh was a bustling river port, with large freighters and sloops coming into and going out of its wharves.

During his first year here Melville took an engineering course at Lansingburgh Academy and graduated with honors. In May of 1839 his first published work, "Fragments from a Writing Desk, No. 1," appeared in the *Democratic Press and Lansingburgh Advertiser.* In that short story he adopted the persona of a proper gentleman who dressed like the dandy Beau Brummell, and won the affections of the local village damsels as no village boy could have. It is thought that the three damsels he referred to may have been local girls he had unsuccessfully courted.

The next month he left on the ship *St. Lawrence* for his first sea voyage, which he later described in *Redburn.* After his return he published his first piece of Gothic fiction in the paper. Then, following a brief stint of schoolteaching at Greenbush and at School-house No. 7 in Brunswick, he sailed out of New Bedford (see entry) on the *Acushnet* for the South Seas. *Typee* and *Omoo* really established Melville as a writer, though these novels received strong criticism from religious groups for their denunciations of the role of Christian missionaries in the South Seas. Melville left Lansingburgh for good after his marriage on August 4, 1847.

The main building of Lansingburgh Academy, which Melville attended in 1839, still stands at 114th Street and Fourth Avenue. It is a two-story Colonial brick building with a dormer roof and a large wooden frame ventilation piece on top.

PENNSYLVANIA

Gettysburg

The **Lincoln Room Museum** (Lincoln Sq. Open daily, spring and fall, 9-5, summer 9-10 P.M. Adm. charged), a privately owned gallery on the top floor of the historic Wills House where Lincoln stayed on November 18, 1863, the night before he delivered the Gettysburg address, concentrates on material relating to his visit and the speech. The focal point is the bedroom where he spent the night and reworked the speech. It is decorated with the original furniture and arranged exactly as it was when he stayed there. A life-size figure of Lincoln sits working at the small table in the middle. When visitors come, the doors of the room are closed and a simulated discussion between Judge Wills and Lincoln relates the events that took place in the house that night. Lincoln had come to say a few words to the widows and orphans at the dedication of Gettysburg Cemetery. After being received, Lincoln was led upstairs by Wills to retire. He then revised the speech he had been preparing in Washington and during his train ride to Gettysburg.

Displays in the large adjoining room concentrate on the address itself. On one wall enlarged copies of all four drafts of the speech are displayed so that they can be easily read. The first (written a night or two before Lincoln left Washington) and the second (one of the first revisions done here at the Wills house) are at the Library of Congress. The third and fourth are owned by university libraries.

One display case has material he used or received during his visit: the key to his room, the original towels and pillows, a telegram from his wife saying that their son Tad was feeling better, and photostats of letters from Judge Wills to Lincoln. Covering one entire wall is a plaque of the address, made with wood from eleven places connected with Lincoln's life—some are from as far off as Kentucky and Illinois, and a few of the letters are even made from an old piece of the White House roof. In addition to many portraits of Lincoln, the museum also has the large leather chair Lincoln sat in during this visit and life-size models of the Lincoln family.

Lincoln delivered the Gettysburg address on November 19, 1863, at Gettysburg National Cemetery, on the spot where the Soldiers National Monument now stands.

Lackawaxen

The **Zane Grey Museum** (at Zane Grey Inn. 2 mi. S of N.Y. State Route 97. 10-4 Tues.-Sun., Apr. 15-end Oct. Adm. charged) reflects the life and works of Zane Grey, who lived here and got his start as a writer when the inn was a solitary cottage on the confluence of the Lackawaxen and Delaware rivers. He had come many times to this wilderness area on fishing trips, and several members of his family owned property nearby. On one visit he met his wife, Lena Roth, who encouraged him in his desire to give up his lucrative Manhattan dental practice and try his hand at writing.

Soon after their marriage, he bought a five-acre plot of land, moved into a little cottage alongside the water, and put away his sign "Dr. Zane Grey, Dentist" and his tools.

Life was hard here for the first four or five years. He made little from writing and used the last of his wife's inheritance for several trips out West to gather details for his novels. In the winters, Grey wrote in the kitchen, warming his fingers at the stove to keep them from freezing. Though his wife was not terribly fond of the area, she labored with him on his writing, teaching him to write smoothly, priming him from grammar texts, and editing and correcting his works. When they ran out of money, she borrowed from her family so they could live while he finished his first novel, *Betty Zane,* a romantic tale of his ancestor's move into the Ohio frontier.

The failure of that work was a great disappointment to him. However, soon after, while he was in New York visiting publishers, he met Buffalo Jones, one of the last of the plainsmen, who was about to make a western expedition and experiment with breeding buffalo with cattle. Grey agreed to come along and write up the experiment. On that trip he gathered material for the first of his many successful Western novels. They went through the Painted Desert of the Navajos with a Mormon caravan, lassoed mountain lions in the Grand Canyon, and lived with rangers and wild-animal hunters.

He returned to Lackawaxen to write his *Heritage of the Desert,* the story of a Mormon girl who escaped from a Mormon colony and fell in love with an Easterner. This novel was successful, but his next, *Riders of the Purple Sage,* sold more than two million copies in the first few years. With his literary success came a change in lifestyle. He hired two secretaries to type out the works which he wrote in longhand on yellow pads. After nine years at Lackawaxen, Grey found he was spending more and more time out West and decided to move there permanently. Though he had houses in Arizona and California he always remained attached to this area and had plans to come back to Lackawaxen to do research for a fishing novel just before he died.

The cottage later became part of the large Zane Grey Inn, operated for many years by Mrs. Helen Johnson, the daughter of the late Alvah Jones, who had introduced Zane Grey to Buffalo Jones.

Though not quite as wild as when Grey lived here, the area is still a favorite with fishermen and hunters. Grey said that an experienced fisherman could cast a line into the Delaware River from the east end of the porch or into the Lackawaxen from the west side. Late in life he described the setting as "very picturesque and a place where the forests abound with game and the streams with fish." He also said that in Lackawaxen he gained his first knowledge of really wild country and had his first happy time since childhood.

Every inch of wall space in the two rooms of the museum is covered with paintings of book jackets, newspaper articles, photographs, and prints. One entire wall is devoted to movie stills from his *Riders of the Purple Sage.* Near the fireplace is the Morris chair where he sat with his lapboard and wrote from early morning to dusk. In addition to many pieces of family furniture are some of his prized possessions: his foot-operated dental drill, his baseball shoes, his children's toys, many of the photographs he took, cowboy hats and riding britches which reflect the years of ranch life out West, and part of his collection of Navajo art. **Old Union Cemetery,** where he and his wife are buried, is just down the road from the inn.

Perkasie

Green Hills Farm (520 Dublin Rd. 1 mi. W of Dublin. Tours of house Mon.-Fri. 10:30 A.M. and 2 P.M. Free), the estate of the late Pearl Buck, is now the headquarters of the Pearl Buck Foundation, which distributes aid to children left throughout Asia by American military servicemen.

In her autobiographical account *My Several Worlds* Pearl Buck describes her years here. She bought the original farmhouse and land in 1934 shortly before her marriage to New York publisher

Richard Walsh. They extensively renovated and enlarged the house and increased the acreage to make a large working farm. Together they raised five adopted children. After Walsh's death in 1960 Pearl Buck adopted four others.

Throughout the main house are many fine Oriental antiques and works of art. The Chinese desk, at which she sat to write *The Good Earth,* is in one of the libraries. In a display room upstairs are many personal mementos and her many honors and awards, including the Nobel Prize. A walkway from the main house leads to the renovated cottage where she had her study. In this light, spacious, airy room she researched and wrote almost all of her later published works. It is as she left it, the light walls covered with Chinese art, and her sculpture studio in the loft. The barn, originally a recreation area for the Buck children and the community, is now office space for the foundation. Miss Buck's simple grave is in a small grove of trees near the main road.

Philadelphia

The **Visitors' Center** (3rd and Chestnut Sts.) and the **Convention and Tourist Bureau** (1525 Kennedy Blvd.) have maps and other material which would be helpful in touring Philadelphia's literary sites.

Independence Hall area: Many of Philadelphia's literary sites are located within five blocks of **Independence National Historical Park,** and can be reached by starting at **Independence Hall** (5th and Chestnut Sts.), where the Second Continental Congress adopted the Declaration of Independence on July 4, 1776.

At the **Christ Church Burial Ground** (5th and Arch Sts.), Benjamin and Deborah Franklin are buried just inside the high wrought-iron fence. Near them are graves of other signers of the Declaration of Independence: Francis Hopkinson, Dr. Benjamin Rush, Joseph Hughes, and George Ross. Franklin died on April 17, 1790. A plaque on the outside of the fence next to his grave has a long list of his accomplishments. Just east, on the grounds of the **Arch Street Friends Meeting House** (between 3rd and 4th Sts. on Arch), America's first novelist, Charles Brockden Brown, is buried. The **Graff House** (7th and Market Sts.) has been reconstructed; here Thomas Jefferson rented an upstairs room and drafted the Declaration of Independence. Downstairs is a simple exhibit illustrating the Declaration of Independence. Upstairs, the parlor and bedroom have been re-created. Jefferson's lap desk and pen set are on a round table in the parlor.

The story of Benjamin Franklin in Philadelphia is told at **Franklin Court** (3rd and Chestnut Sts.), which has a partial reconstruction of the court as it was in Franklin's time, an outdoor skeletal model of the house he designed and had built, and multimedia exhibits on his life. Many details about the house, which stood approximately where the skeletal frame is now, are known from correspondence between Franklin and his wife Deborah during the ten years he was in London. Excerpts from some of those letters are carved into some of the stones in the courtyard. It is possible to look through glass-covered openings to see some of the original foundations of the house which archaeologists have laid bare. Their findings and the surviving written descriptions were used to reconstruct this section of Franklin Court.

In the 1760s Franklin contracted a master carpenter to build a large house to stand in a quiet green deep in the middle of the block. Franklin had to leave for England while the house was under construction, and unfortunately his wife died before he was able to return. When he came back his daughter and her family had moved into the house and he added an extension for himself. It was there that he probably wrote his *Autobiography*. At that time his print shop, no longer standing, was located at 139 Market Street.

One major attraction of the museum is the Franklin Exchange, a series of simulated telephone hookups with famous European and American writers and statesmen who have made statements about the effect Franklin had on their lives. Among those who may be "called" are John Adams, Thomas Jefferson, Herman Melville, John Keats, Lord Byron, Mark Twain, and D. H. Lawrence. In addition, there are a number of exhibits on the various roles Franklin played: diplomat, statesman, printer, author, scientist, inventor. An adjoining gallery has copies of well-known portraits of Franklin at various ages and some original Franklin furniture and reproductions of furniture of the period.

Edgar Allan Poe's haunts on **Chestnut Street** are beyond the back entrance of Franklin Court. Poe spent a lot of time in the area between Independence Hall and the river. His historic meeting with Dickens occurred on Chestnut Street somewhere between 4th and 5th Streets. *Graham's,* where he worked as an editor in the early 1840s (see Poe House entry, below), stood on the southwest corner of Chestnut and 3rd Streets. Many of the buildings he knew in his ramblings here still stand, though in his time the spacious greens between them did not exist. At 2nd and Dock was the Merchant's Exchange where he came daily for his mail. *Burton's Gentleman's Magazine,* which he also worked for, was next door.

Another cluster of literary sites is located west of Washington Square. The small walled-in **Mikveh Israel Cemetery** (between 8th and 9th Sts. on Spruce) is where philanthropist Rebecca Gratz, whom Sir Walter Scott came to know and admire, is buried. He patterned the Rebecca of *Ivanhoe* after her. One block away, at **222 South 8th Street,** Bronson Alcott, social reformer and father of Louisa May, operated a school in 1830 (see Concord, Massachusetts).

Slightly farther west at **922 Spruce Street** is the red brick townhouse where Sarah Josepha Hale lived when she came to Philadelphia to become editor of *Godey's Lady's Book* (see Newport, New Hampshire). At **913 Pine Street** was the home of Owen Wister, grandson of Shakespearean actress Fanny Kemble and author of *The Virginian.* Around the corner is the **Henry George School** (413 South 10th St.), the birthplace of Henry George, economist, reformer, and author of *Progress and Poverty;* the school offers courses in economics and social reform. Now part of Pierce Junior College is a three-story building at **1426 Pine Street** that was the boyhood home of the eminent Shakespearean scholar, Horace Howard Furness.

Elsewhere in Philadelphia: The **Edgar Allan Poe House** (530 North 7th St. Open Mon.-Fri. 10-5, Sat. and Sun. 2-5. Closed hols. Adm. charged), a quaint Colonial structure with fresh green lawn and garden, is a contrast to the commercial buildings surrounding it. In Poe's day the "rose-covered cottage," as it was then called, was part of a well-to-do Quaker settlement called Spring Garden, then on the outskirts of the city. Poe came to Philadelphia in the summer of 1839 when he took over as editor of *Burton's Gentleman's Magazine.* After living at various rooming houses at 4th and Arch, 12th and Arch, 16th and Locust, and 25th and Fairmount Streets, Poe, his wife Virginia, and his mother-in-law and aunt, Mrs. Clemm, were very relieved to settle in at the little house. Here Poe was close to the center of town and the publishing houses and yet could stroll out into the countryside of Fairmount by merely heading west on Spring Garden Street.

His contemporaries have described the cottage as set back from the street amid luxuriant grape arbors and other vines, with an enormous pear tree, later felled by lightning, shading the porch at the west side. Here the family retreated from the hot afternoon sun, and Poe often sat to read and write. ("The Gold-Bug" is among the stories he is thought to have written here.) At other times Poe would sit here playing with his cats while the sound of Virginia's harp could be heard through the window. The opening to the cellar here is described in his story "The Tale of the Gray Tad-pole." Some feel that the spacious cellar with its brick wall must be the setting for "The Black Cat" or "The Cask of Amontillado," since the foundations for the house's fireplaces are here.

The front entrance opens onto a spacious stairwell which separates the restored Poe house from a newer building which adjoins it. Materials on Poe and the house are on display in the more recent structure. A door to the left of the front entrance leads into the small parlor of the original house. Here in this low, twelve-foot-square room Poe wrote and entertained his friends. While Poe worked in one of the chairs his favorite cats, Cissie and Muddie, curled up in front of the cast-iron stove, and Mrs. Clemm sat with her sewing box in the corner between the fireplace and the side table. Mrs. Clemm, who took care of all the practical matters of the household, served as housekeeper, cook, and messenger. Often Poe sat up all night in his chair, attempting to perfect his stories, motivated in part at least by Virginia's medical bills, which lay piled up on the piano. On the west wall of the parlor a small glass plate covers the carving "Death to the" that was uncovered during the restoration of the house. Since biographers mention his penchant for carving and sketching on walls, and also because most of his works of this period have the theme of death, it seems reasonable to assume that these cryptic words were carved by Poe. He is known to have written on his bedroom wall in Richmond, at the University of Virginia, and at West Point. At one home in New York Poe was supposedly reprimanded for carving his initials in a highly prized parlor mantelpiece.

A narrow stairway between the kitchen and parlor leads to Poe's bedroom and study on the second floor. Here in his study he sometimes worked at a simple little desk while sitting in a large rocker. Above him Virginia often lay sick, and in their last years here she was even unable to make her way downstairs to strum on the harp or play the piano. The other upstairs room was occupied by Mrs. Clemm.

These bedrooms, now restored, were much more sparsely furnished when the Poes lived here. As Virginia's hemorrhages became worse Mrs. Clemm found it necessary to sell the piano and other furniture piecemeal to supplement Poe's meager earnings, in order to pay Virginia's medical bills. By the time they left for New York there were few pieces left, and Mrs. Clemm settled the unpaid rent by giving the landlord their kitchen chairs, horsehair sofa, and Poe's favorite red carpet.

During the two years he lived here Poe refined the craft of the short story. Among the works written here are "The Gold-Bug," "The Black Cat," "The Masque of the Red Death," "The Mystery of Marie Roget," "The Murders in the Rue Morgue," "The Pit and the Pendulum," "The Tell-Tale Heart," "Ligeia," and "The Raven." Though he received only one hundred dollars for "The Gold-Bug" when it came out in the *Dollar Newspaper,* the publisher had to issue more than three hundred thousand extra copies to meet the demand. In 1841 Poe became editor of *Graham's Magazine,* a noted literary journal which succeeded *Burton's Gentleman's Magazine.* During his time there the readership increased from less than five thousand to more than fifty thousand.

Though these years were a period of success, Poe also knew despair. While he had become respected as an editor and literary critic, he also saw his young wife Virginia gradually succumb to consumption. Then there was also his own dependence on narcotics and liquor. How much of that weakness caused him to lose his position at *Graham's* and take off for New York (see New York City, Bronx), poverty-stricken, is a matter of speculation. Poe is said to have left Philadelphia with nothing except his books under one arm and his two cats under the other.

Though the **Rosenbach Foundation Museum** (2010 Delancey Place. Open 2-5, June-July, Mon.-Fri.; Sept.-May, Tues.-Sun. Closed hols. and Aug. Adm. charged), the former home of Philip H. Rosenbach and his brother, Dr. A. S. W. Rosenbach, emphasizes their collection of rare books and manuscripts, many rooms of this double townhouse are filled with priceless antiques and artwork as well. The focal point of the museum, at least from a literary point of view, is the original autograph manuscript of James Joyce's *Ulysses* in the front hallway. Dr. Rosenbach bought it in 1924 from John Quinn, a New York lawyer who invested in books and manuscripts by promising writers in the early twenties. This was the copy Joyce sent episode by episode to *The Little Review.* In all, the museum has 100,000 original manuscript items and 25,000 volumes of rare books. Each year four special manuscript exhibitions are compiled, usually each on a particular author or theme.

On the third floor are two separate libraries of rare books. Highlights of the European section are the first editions in both Spanish and English of *Don Quixote,* a set of Milton's documents, Milton's personal copy of the works of Thucydides, and Boswell's copy of his *Life of Samuel Johnson.* In addition to many presentation copies there are displays of the John Tenniel illustrations of Lewis Carroll's *Alice in Wonderland.* Also here is a famous love letter from Keats to Fanny Brawne, and sections of *Nicholas Nicklehy* and other Dickens manuscripts. Among the Conrad material are a rough working copy of *Lord Jim* and the complete manuscripts of *The Nigger of the Narcissus, Almayer's Folly,* and *Lord Jim.*

The American Room is devoted to rare pieces in American history and literature. The collection includes an American Indian Bible printed in 1640 and thought to be the earliest book printed in what is now the United States, and some original letters of Emily Dickinson. In addition there are many eighteenth- and nineteenth-century histories of individual states, books about women, and books about frontier life.

One room is a re-creation of poet Marianne Moore's Greenwich Village apartment in New York, complete with the contents she donated to the museum. In the entranceway some interesting documents are displayed: letters she received from Lawrence Durrell and Allen Ginsberg and the working manuscript of her famous poem about the Brooklyn Bridge, "Granite and Steel," with comments in different colors to illustrate the various stages she went through in revising it. In addition, Maurice Sendak has donated all of his original drawings to the museum and some are on permanent display.

There are also a number of other pieces with literary associations. Near the downstairs hallway is an oil painting made from an illustration of the *Old Curiosity Shop* in London. On the first landing is a watercolor by poet William Blake. In the alcove behind it is one of Herman Melville's Gothic-style bookcases, similar to the one on display at his home in Pittsfield, Massachusetts (see entry). Inside is the copy of *Moby Dick* which Melville dedicated to Hawthorne and presented to him.

West Philadelphia: Clarence H. P. Clark Park (43rd St. and Baltimore Ave.) has the only known **statue of Charles Dickens.** There the bronze Dickens sits in a high-backed chair gazing pensively at "Little Nell," who stands below him alongside the granite base. In his will Dickens stated that he did not want to be the subject of any monument or memorial. American sculptor Frank Edwin Elwell, unaware of that stipulation, did the sculpture, which was exhibited in London and at the Chicago World's Fair in 1893 before being purchased by the city's park commission and set up here in 1901.

RHODE ISLAND

Block Island

The **Palatine Graves** (E off Dickens Pt., SW side of island), associated with John Greenleaf Whittier's poem "The Palatine Light," are marked by a memorial erected in 1728, and rededicated in 1947 with the inscription, "To commemorate the twenty passengers of the 1720–55 wreck which gave rise to the Fire Ship legend of Block Island. (The exact date of the wreck is in dispute.)

The Palatine had long been an island legend when Whittier composed his poem in 1867. His friend James Hazard of Rhode Island had written him a version of it and Whittier related the tale as he imagined old Block Islanders would tell it. In the poem, the *Palatine* crashes onto the rocky coast of the island. As soon as the boat reaches the shore, scavengers come and take the valuables, having no regard for the dead. The survivors are then taken to the home of Simon Ray, and the dead buried on his property, where the Palatine marker now stands.

One version of the legend is that of a ship which came over in the 1700s full of Dutch merchants from the German Palatinate. The ship never made it to Philadelphia, its destination, because of many storms. Eventually, unable to reach land, the crew mutinied, killed the captain, and held the passengers until they paid high prices for their food. Those who had no money starved. Then, when they were in sight of land, the crew took the lifeboats and escaped with the money and valuables. The ship was then allowed to toss and turn until it crashed against the shore at Sandy Point.

Another version says that the islanders towed the boat as far as Beach Cove, and when it began to drift out in a gale they set it on fire, fearing that if it blew off shore it could be an obstruction to other ships. An embellishment of that version says that one woman who had hoarded valuables and refused to leave the ship drifted away on the burning vessel, and that her screams could be heard on shore. Still another version blames the burning on a local arsonist who had just previously set the island's windmill on fire. The supernatural appearance of the burning ship over the waves has been referred to as the "Palatine Light," or "Fire Ship"; the light is said to have reappeared annually for years after the event. That myth became a popular motif of writers around 1875, although not always specifically related to that. In the poem Whittier said that on many a moonless night one could see the blazing wreck of the *Palatine*. Some experts explain it as a natural phenomenon, a glow which appeared from time to time due to huge reflections of schools of fish which islanders would have been watching for.

One island historian found evidence of a ship named *Palatine* which stopped off in 1745 and left between seventeen and twenty passengers in diseased or dying condition. These people were nursed by the islanders and the dead were buried in the Palatine Graves. According to local histories other aged islanders remember stories of invalid passengers from the *Palatine* being cared for at Simon Ray's home. One particular old-timer recalls his parents speaking of a "Dutch Kattern" or "Long Kate," a survivor of the wreck who married a slave; in this version of the story, the crew of the ship starved the passengers for money, and there was no burning.

Newport

The **Old Stone Mill** or **Round Tower** (Touro Park, Mill St. off Bellevue Ave.) is often associated with Longfellow's famous poem "A Skeleton in Armor," a ballad based partly on a translation of an old German legend and partly on local tradition. Longfellow, like others in the nineteenth century, thought that this circular stone tower had been built by twelfth-century Norsemen, since a skeleton with a metal plate on his chest had been found in the nearby Fall River. Longfellow had seen the skeleton soon after it was found and assumed it was one of the Vikings who had come here somewhere between the tenth and twelfth centuries. He also based his views on studies done by archaeologists of his time who had come to the conclusion that the tower had been built by Norsemen as a religious settlement. Another tradition held that the tower was part of a seventeenth-century windmill on land once belonging to Benedict Arnold. The latest evidence suggests that the tower was a mill built by colonists in the 1660s.

In the poem, Longfellow asks the skeleton to explain his presence. He confesses that he was an old Viking who built the lofty tower which "stands looking seaward." Later, it was discovered that the skeleton was an Indian who had been wearing a breastplate of English origin.

In another poem, "The Jewish Cemetery at Newport," Longfellow wrote about the old cemetery at the corner of Kay Street and Bellevue Avenue.

Newport was a gathering place for other writers in the nineteenth century. Helen Hunt Jackson, author of the novel *Ramona,* ran Dame's Boarding Home, where members of the literary set lived.

Julia Ward Howe, usually remembered only as the author of "The Battle Hymn of the Republic," started the Town and Country Club, a literary group which counted among its members John Greenleaf Whittier. Bret Harte, usually associated with California, came here to live for five years after he had become a successful writer, and was lionized by the cultured elite of Newport. His poems "A Greyport Legend" and "A Newport Romance" were set here.

Providence

The **Whitman House** (88 Benefit St. Not open to public) is often pointed out as a literary landmark since it was the home of poet Sarah Helen Whitman, who was engaged for a short time to Edgar Allan Poe.

Poe first caught a glimpse of Mrs. Whitman one hot summer night in 1845, as she stood in her doorway trying to get a breath of fresh air. He had heard of her, since she was considered the poetess of Providence and often had groups of people in to discuss mysticism and idealism. She had heard of him, since she corresponded with many literary figures of the day. Three years after that summer night, and after considerable correspondence and a number of poems had been exchanged between the two, he returned to Providence and proposed.

Though her parents, who came from one of the best-known families in the city, protested the marriage, the two often met in the cloistered recesses of the Athenaeum (251 Benefit St. Open Mon.-Fri. 8:30-5:30; Sat. 9:30-5:30) near the house. Poe proposed and a marriage covenant was written, only to be broken at the insistence of the Whitman family, who refused to sanction his dissolute habits after he had repeatedly fallen from grace. *Last Letters of Edgar Allan Poe to Sarah Helen Whitman* (1909), collected by James A. Harrison, covers the period of their courtship.

After the engagement was broken Poe left the city depressed and passed out from a heavy dose of laudanum on the trip back to New York where he was living. The effect Mrs. Whitman had on him can be realized by reading his poem "To Helen," which he said had been inspired by her. Some feel that Mrs. Whitman was also his "Annabel Lee," though most Poe experts feel that Annabel Lee is his dead wife Virginia.

After his death Mrs. Whitman wrote *Poe and his Critics* (1860), which in addition to being a defense of Poe against his critics, such as the Reverend Rufus W. Griswold, who had made slanderous charges against him, was considered a brilliant critical analysis of his works.

Brown University's John Hay Library (Prospect St. Open Mon.-Fri., Sept.-May, 8:30-5; June-Aug. from 9 A.M.) has a special collection of Lincoln manuscripts and the noted Harris collection of American poetry and plays. The University's **Annmary Brown Memorial** (Brown St., N of Charles Field St. Open Mon.-Fri. 9-5) has a fine collection of rare books from 1450 to 1500 and American portraits.

VERMONT

Brattleboro

Naulakha (take Black Mountain Rd. off US 5, N of Brattleboro; Black Mountain Rd. becomes Kipling Rd.; take left at fork in road. House is ½ mile from that point), where Rudyard Kipling spent nine years, has long been a popular literary shrine. Though now *privately owned and no longer open to the public,* the house is visible from the road.

Kipling came to the area from London as the husband of a native Vermonter, Caroline Balestier, the sister of his good friend Charles Wolcott Balestier, with whom he had collaborated on a novel called *The Naulakha: A Story of East and West,* in which a midwestern American goes to India in search of a famous necklace known as the Naulakha, meaning nine "lakhs" or 900,000 rupees. Balestier supposedly typed the manuscript while his friend Kipling paced the floor of his London flat and dictated to him.

Just before his marriage Kipling made a brief trip home to see his parents in Lahore, the city where he passed the early part of his life, and where he began his literary career with the *Civil and Military Gazette* of Lahore. At that time, he rediscovered the Naulakha Pavilion there. He described the pavilion as "aching in the sun" amid the city of domes and bastions. Kipling returned abruptly to the continent after learning of Wolcott's sudden death. Soon after, he married Caroline Balestier and found himself building an American Naulakha near her childhood home in the rolling Vermont Hills.

Bliss Cottage, where the Kiplings lived while Naulakha was being built, was originally located on the left side of Kipling Road near the campus of Experiment for International Living. It is now a few hundred yards eastward on the other side of the road and has been considerably remodeled. Kipling's first daughter Josephine was born at the cottage during a fierce blizzard in December 1892 and spent her first few months sleeping in a trunk tray. Dr. James Conland, who came up in his hooded sleigh to deliver the child, later became a good friend and inspired Kipling to write *Captains Courageous.*

Unfortunately, the trees and shrubs have grown up so much around the two-story frame bungalow that in summer you can only get a glimpse of Naulakha. Kipling described the long house with its back against the hillside "like a boat on the flank of a distant wave." All of its rooms faced a beautiful view across the Connecticut Valley and New Hampshire where Mount Monadnock breaks the horizon "like a giant thumbnail pointing heavenward." At the time the house was built there were very few trees around it. A winding drive curved around to an entrance at the back.

According to *Literary Haunts and Homes* by Theodore F. Wolfe (Lippincott, 1899) a wide veranda opened out onto Kipling's garden at the southern end. His study was also at this end of the house. There he worked a few hours each morning, refusing to see anyone. During his years here he wrote his book of poetry, *The Seven Seas,* which marked him as a major poet, many of the stories of the *Jungle Books,* and the whole of *Captains Courageous,* his novel of New England fishermen.

He spent his afternoons strolling through the beautiful open countryside, and often took a daily walk to the post office in Dummerston. Since he hated horses he often rode a bicycle for longer trips. The figure of a short man in a gray suit and broad-brimmed gray hat perched up on a two-wheeler was a familiar sight to many in the area.

Kipling's reputation among the local townspeople was one of a recluse. Although many thought him eccentric, he was considered an asset to the area since he was famous and financially independent. Vermont was a strange place to one who had grown up with the British consciousness of class, and his class consciousness showed in his relationship with his Vermont neighbors. In addition, the building of a strange house, which some described as an ark, did not help his image. Because of his lifestyle he was rumored to have great wealth. The Kiplings hired English house servants and an English coachman dressed in a red-coat livery, and they dressed formally for dinner. As his income and fame grew, Kipling felt the need to build a private post office, and this further alienated him from his fellow Vermonters. One of his few friends in the area was Dr. James Conland, with whom he often took trips to Gloucester, Massachusetts, at that time declining as a sailing center, to sail and fish. Here he collected local color for *Captains Courageous*. The opening scene with Harvey Cheyne being swept into the water by a huge wave and then rescued by the dory of a codfish schooner is taken from Kipling's first experience there. Many of the old stories and legends came from the time the two spent in old wharf restaurants.

Mrs. Kipling ran everything at Naulakha, just as she was to do later at Burwash, the English estate they built in Sussex. She handled all of the financial affairs and the secretarial work, and supervised the farm as well. Kipling was known to have no use for details of everyday living and when asked about any matter on his property, except for an occasional pet project which might catch his fancy, would retort coldly, "Ask my wife." He once described privacy as a blessed state in which one hangs on to as few persons and things as possible.

In order to protect his seclusion a single passage led to that study on the south end of the house. Newspapermen and other visitors could never get through because his wife guarded the door. He became more and more famous as he lived here, and while neighbors respected his privacy, he was constantly sought by the press, so much so that when the Kiplings decided to return to England permanently they searched carefully for a secluded place. His decision to return to England may have been due, in part, to strained relations with his wife's brother Beatty Balestier, apparently an alcoholic and ne'er-do-well. The Kiplings left Brattleboro after a much publicized lawsuit over some property Caroline Kipling was to have received from him.

Ferrisburg

Rokeby (on US 7, 2 mi. N of Vergennes. Open May 15-Oct. 15, Mon.-Sat. 9:30-5, Sun. 11-5. Closed Tues. Adm. charged), the lifelong home of Rowland Robinson (1833–1900), illustrator and writer, is now open as a museum of nineteenth-century Vermont farm life. The Robinsons were enlightened, well-read Quaker farmers who kept a prosperous one-thousand-acre sheep farm with a dairy and orchards. The library and parlor often served as reading and meeting places for Quakers in this part of Vermont. Those rooms and, in fact, the rest of the house, are almost exactly as they were over a century ago.

Robinson, who turned to writing after he became blind, spent most of his time composing and studying in the library. On the high desk is the grooved board on which he wrote. Most of his original manuscripts are in folders in bookcases lining the walls. The Robinsons' complete collections of various magazines dating from around 1840 to 1900 are being catalogued and sorted. Some of them will stay here and others will be donated to libraries who need to complete their collections. In addition to the old books and periodicals there are thousands of family letters detailing Vermont farm life during that time. On the walls are a number of old family portraits, and bric-a-brac abounds in the library, as it does all over the house.

Small oils of local scenes hang on the wall in the adjoining sitting room. In the rear is the huge old farm kitchen with the original furniture. Prior to the Civil War this house was an important stop on the Underground Railroad. In the small east room just back of the kitchen, marks indicate the spot where the tunnel entrance was located. Floorboards were lifted and slaves were sent through a passageway that ended in the nearby woods. They would escape by night and try to reach the Canadian border by morning.

All over the house are illustrations done by Robinson and his daughter Rachel, who became a successful commercial artist in New York. Her upstairs bedroom, with artwork lining the walls, is as she left it in 1910. The back bedrooms, with their low ceilings and small arched windows, have the original rope beds. This is where the slaves stayed while in hiding. The room with the double bed, trunk, and desk was described in Robinson's book *Out of Bondage.*

Ripton

The **Homer Noble Farm** (2 mi. E of Ripton. Take unpaved road in woods next to Robert Frost Wayside area), where Robert Frost spent his summers from the late 1930s until 1962, is open as a memorial to him. Frost spent his first summer in the area in 1939 when he came to lecture at the summer session of Middlebury's Bread Loaf School of English and stayed at a faculty cottage a few miles away on the campus. He was then at a turning point in his life. He had recently lost his wife Elinor after forty-two years of marriage, and had pulled up long-standing roots in Amherst and moved on to Harvard.

The next summer, at age 66, he bought the Homer Noble Farm, which then consisted of several hundred acres of woods, fields, and brooks in addition to the farmhouse, the cabin which he converted into his studio and living quarters, and a few outbuildings. The cabin, set up in the fields several hundred yards beyond the farmhouse, is as he left it at the end of his last summer there. Most of his later works were written in the front room, where he sat before the fieldstone fireplace in his Morris chair with a lap desk. He bought the chair in 1897 when he was an undergraduate and took it with him as he moved around from place to place. The floor-to-ceiling bookcases hold the library which he often used for reference. In the small back room are his bed, simple desk, lamp, and chair. Just outside the high bedroom window is a beautiful grove of white birches.

As soon as he purchased the farm Frost convinced the Morrisons, his close friends from Cambridge, to rent the farmhouse from him and provide him with meals. Since he had a hired man to help run the farm, he was able to devote himself to his writing and enjoy farm chores on the side. Mrs. Kathleen Johnston Morrison, once a student of Frost's at Bryn Mawr, acted as his secretary from 1939 until his death in 1962. She helped him manage his personal affairs, literary and otherwise. She writes of their years at Ripton in her book *Robert Frost: A Pictorial Chronicle* (Holt, Rinehart and Winston, 1974). Professor Morrison, her husband, was a member of Harvard's English Department at the same time Frost was there, and both were involved with Bread Loaf in the summer. Thus Frost always had companionship, as well as secretarial and practical help when needed.

While he lived here, Frost had a habit of buying up neighboring properties and renovating the houses, something he had done before in other areas of New England. He would draw up designs for renovation, and then hire a man to work along with him. Then he rented out the places to friends or put his children in them for the summer. He also built up the Homer Noble farmhouse by adding an ell and several rooms. With his passion for baseball he became very involved with the annual Bread Loaf faculty baseball game, which was held in the fields here at the farm. He took the event very seriously and spent days inspecting the hayfield to see if rocks were removed and the surface was smooth enough for play.

Frost's usual pattern was to work from ten until three in the cabin, interrupted only by a basket lunch brought up from the main house. Late afternoons were spent on farm chores such as tending the garden or chopping wood. Each evening he had dinner with the Morrisons and was often joined by their guests or his own. Many times he would take visitors up to his cabin for conversation that lasted well into the morning hours. His dog Gillie was constantly at his side and followed his pattern of late night walks, staying up until the early morning hours and rising late.

With the Morrisons taking care of the practical side of his life Frost was able to devote himself to his work. During the first decade here he wrote four books of poetry: *A Witness Tree, A Masque of Reason, Steeple Bush,* and *A Masque of Mercy.* The Morrisons made sure that his poetry came first and that he was not consumed by his own practical affairs or by the intrusion of visitors who happened by.

Robert Frost Memorial Drive, a fourteen-mile route through the woods, farmlands, and mountains which were so much a part of Frost's life and poetry, has recently been dedicated. It starts at the junction of US 7 and State Route 125 in East Middlebury. At the little hamlet of Ripton (several miles east on Route 125), is Ripton Gorge. "The Bridge of Flowers," with its flower boxes, is mentioned in several poems. Two miles east of Ripton is the **Robert Frost Wayside** area, where the Robert Frost Interpretive Trail begins. Seven of his poems are mounted on plaques on the three-quarter-mile stretch of State Route 125 between the Wayside area and the Bread Loaf campus, where yellow Victorian buildings stand out against the rolling green hills. On campus is a large inn, the Little Theatre where Frost often lectured, the library, and a number of houses and cottages.

INDEX